INTUITIVE

SPEAKING HER TRUTH

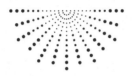

The Art of Grace

PUBLISHING HOUSE

To all those who are not yet ready to speak their truth.

CONTENTS

INTRODUCTION

For thousands of years, women's stories have been hidden, shunned, pushed down, ignored, and unable to be acknowledged. The same can be said for our INTUITION. For thousands of years we have hidden, shied away from, and pushed down our own thoughts. We have ignored them, unable to acknowledge that we truly can trust that inner knowing.

What is it that makes us not trust ourselves?

Social or Religious constraints? Family, Partners, Friends, Lifestyles? Anything outside of us can, and does, affect who we truly are. We doubt our own thoughts, we think "they" know better, and we begin to believe all that is put in front of us. External forces take over and our intuition slips into the shadows. We lose it for a time—there is a way back.

We are all born with the wonderful power of INTUITION—we are all intuitive. In these pages, women share their range of experiences and the lessons they learnt to show you how you too can reconnect with yourself, with your inner knowing, with your gut feelings, and with your TRUE self—your INTUITION.

It is not enough for us to just meditate, concentrate, or think positively—there is more. You my dear, have the power to this intuitive self. There is the self-worth, the self-trust, the innate knowing, and the power to connect with it. Being able to not only connect to your intuitive self, but they too will show you how to use your voice and speak your own truth!

The Art of Grace Publishing House is changing the narrative around women sharing their voices and has created a platform for women to share their voices and leave a legacy in this world that allows them to show others what is possible.

If you are ready to share your journey, reach out.

We all seem to lose our connection at one point, yet we can all get it back. Go now, read and allow their words to be your guide back to your true self, or a lovely reminder of how you can find your true self and utilise your intuition to guide you on your next chapter of life.

Much Love
B xx

1

PATTY OLIVER

PERSONAL POWER!

I was being led down a long, empty hallway in the medical building. There was absolutely no one in sight, as it was late on a Friday afternoon of a long holiday weekend, so everyone probably bailed early. I could feel the silence, yet the pounding of my heart was echoing in my head, along with the clip-clop of her shoes as the nurse, clutching her clipboard and walking quickly with her eyes down as if to avoid eye contact, hastily directed me to a room at the end of the corridor. I was probably the last checkbox on her list before she, too, could start her holiday weekend. "I'll make this brief," she said bluntly. "You have breast cancer. We don't know what stage, we don't know how invasive, but you have breast cancer. You'll be assigned a medical team that will consist of a surgeon, a radiologist, and an oncologist who will direct your cancer treatment program."

I honestly don't remember what else she said after that. Because I KNEW. I knew I had breast cancer, it had been coming to me for weeks. It's like The Universe was sending me messages left and right to make it beyond obvious that I was about to enter a crisis. I suddenly started seeing articles about breast cancer. Ads for cancer centers were cropping up in my space. I would randomly drop things out of my right hand (the tumor was under my right arm); I had an unshakeable tiredness in my body that was never alleviated by sleep. More than once, a box or book would come flying off a shelf when I walked by. A friend I hadn't spoken to in years called out of the blue to tell me about a good friend of hers who was just diagnosed with breast cancer. I mean, what were the odds? Source was sending me a very clear message.

This had been in mid-May of 2007. Then one night I was woken up out of deep sleep. I was laying on my left side with my right arm draped along my right side. My then-husband was sound asleep next to me. I felt a weird "twinge" in my right armpit, almost like a mild electrical zap. I lifted my arm to try to shake it off and laid it back along my right side, but then another mild zap. So, I lifted my right arm and with my left hand, as if divinely guided, went straight to a lump deep in my right armpit. I couldn't have located it any more directly. "There it is...there's the cancer," I whispered to myself in calm confirmation. And the thing was, I wasn't scared. Because I knew. I also knew that this was my deciding moment. My entire future rested on my very next decision. It wasn't about how to beat the cancer, because I knew I would. My decision was about how I was going to start taking my power back. It was in giving my power away over the years that contributed to my body producing breast cancer, and no one will ever convince me otherwise.

For as long as I can remember, I never truly believed in myself. I never felt fully heard or understood. I preferred to stay in the background, letting someone else lead all aspects of my life. This belief started in very early childhood where I was much happier and more comfortable just playing with my dolls in my room. Sometimes I would even play board games with myself. I'd be the dog, the racecar, AND the wheelbarrow in Monopoly! All were playing against each other with me as the ultimate director. Even when I had all the playing pieces, I was still too darn nice and no one "player" ever hoarded all the money and properties. Because, well, that wasn't fair and that wasn't nice. And that is how I led most of my life: fair and nice. I just felt everyone knew better than me; my mom, my dad, my brother, my friends, and then eventually my husbands (yes, plural).

As I grew, boys entered my life, probably way too soon. In the theater, I found something I loved to do (and was actually good at!). I now realise that I always had a boyfriend because I needed the attention, and I always put them first. In doing so, I would often give up theater roles, miss attending cast parties, I turned down an opportunity to study theater, heck, I even declined a job offer in the industry because my then fiancé said that was his area of expertise and he didn't want to end up competing with me. So, I simply said "okay" and gave up a job that could have put me on an entirely new trajectory. No one could believe I just rolled over and accepted his ultimatum, but to me, it was "fair and nice" and I didn't want to risk losing the guy I loved. The irony of it all is that I eventually did lose him about four years later and was devastated. It was not long after that I met my soon-to-be second husband, my soulmate.

He was the perfect gentlemen in every way. He had a laugh that came from deep in his belly and you could often hear him cackling with joy from the other room. His happiness was infectious and everyone loved him, especially me. We found our best friend in each other (something I highly recommend you look for in a partner) and it was without a doubt, a pivotal relationship for me. He loved me unquestionably and unabashedly just as I was. He made me feel that yes, I was worthy of love in every way. I think that was the intention of this relationship, to help me wake up and realize my own worth. A few short years into the relationship, he was diagnosed with colon cancer, and suddenly I was plunged into caretaker mode, which I did without hesitation. The next few years were full of doctors, surgeries, chemotherapy, and healing, but neither of us complained. I was, however, in denial. I never thought he could be taken from me, we had only just found each other, how could this be happening? But it was, and slowly but surely cancer took over. We were only together for seven years, but it was the most meaningful and deeply joyful period of my life. That was 21 years ago, and I still sense him around me at times. The grief of losing him was unbearable and took me years to overcome.

But life is meant for the living. Even though it seemed incredibly unfair that the person I loved most in the world had been taken from me, apparently I still had work to do in further relationships during this lifetime. After all, I was only 35 at the time. About six months after he passed, God sent me the man who would become husband number three. I met him at a business networking event (I had a business making corporate gift baskets for companies). The funny thing is that I didn't really want to attend this event, but something kept nagging me in the back of my mind to go; "only for an hour", I told myself. Well, that was long enough to bump into a new man. We exchanged business cards. A few months later we started dating, and within a year we were married.

So I know what you're thinking as you're reading this because I'm thinking the same thing now that I'm reliving all of this! "Why did she keep jumping into marriages? Geez, take a few years off to recalibrate!" Well, I would certainly give that advice now...but at the time, I just couldn't see my life complete without a husband to take care of, or one who would take care of me. The problem was, I was on auto-pilot, thinking (like I always did) that I wasn't enough, I couldn't do it on my own, and that I needed someone to tell me what I should do and how to do it. Boy did I find that in husband number three! Not that he's a bad person by any means, but he is definitely a leader who liked to be in control at all times. He had it all figured out, and I was simply along for the ride. Down I went – I was miserable. Feeling unheard and misunderstood again, like I had my entire life. Now that I clear karma for a living, I know without a doubt that these were my biggest karmic patterns I came here to resolve: lack of confidence in myself and over-giving in romantic relationships. Until I found my confidence and stopped being a doormat in relationships, the universe continued to send me men that made me feel that way.

We were constantly arguing, and I felt more and more unhappy, sad, lost, angry, frustrated, and completely powerless to change it, which is an excellent recipe for attracting lack of abundance by the way (this includes poor health and poor relationships, as well as financially poor). I wore my misery on my shirtsleeve, trying desperately to feel heard, but it didn't work. I was one sad, emotional mess; my body hurt, being filled with only desperation, sadness, and resentment. All this piled on top of the endless grief I had never fully resolved over losing my second husband. One thing I did know was that I couldn't continue like that; I told myself "I'm going to put myself in an early grave if I keep this up. My body simply won't hold up to all this emotional upheaval!" I had just turned 42, one year after having my second child. This is where my chapter started, with me learning that I had breast cancer.

It all came flooding into my mind in those few moments after I found the lump. I knew I had it for a reason, which was for me to discover my own empowerment. I also knew that I would beat it and go on to do great things for the rest of my life. I decided right then and there to give up on my emotional downward spiral and work through my grief. I would put it in a place where it could no longer plague me, allow me to grow a backbone, and start taking my happiness into my own hands because I would never find it in anyone else. I was fully capable of living my life on my terms, but now was time to actually choose it.

The first action I took was to see my doctor immediately for the next steps. I was seen by his physician's assistant, who nonchalantly said "I see so many lumps and they never turn out to be anything!" She walked over, gave a few presses of her hand, shrugged, and said "I don't feel anything, you're fine" and began washing her hands. I sat there dumbfounded for a moment, and for a split second I thought about agreeing with her – after all, she knows better than me, right? Nope – this is the new me! "No you need to come back and look again, you missed it," I said, "give me your hand and I'll show you!" I guided her hand deep into my right armpit. "Hmmm. Okay, there might be something there so I'll set up an ultrasound." She clearly was unimpressed. My goodness if I had listened to her, I might not be here today to write about this... (it is worth mentioning that about two weeks after my diagnosis, she called me specifically to apologize for her behavior).

After the ultrasound, I was led down the hall where I started this chapter. So now began my journey of a myriad of decisions that demanded empowerment or that I will be at the mercy of what everyone else thought I should do (another recipe for lasting unhappiness!). My official diagnosis was stage 2 triple-negative breast cancer with no lymph node involvement. In 2007 there were not many options for this highly aggressive form of breast cancer. So I decided on the extreme: double mastectomy with reconstruction and implants.

It just seemed logical to me to remove both breasts. I know some women have a hard time with this, but I never defined myself by my gender or my body parts. While it doesn't guarantee 100% nonrecurrence, it comes pretty darn close. I also opted to have chemotherapy. Even though this didn't improve my odds a ton, I felt it better to have than to not. I took the most "poisonous" part of the chemo cocktail for the first 4 weeks, choosing to be brought to my knees once a week for 4 weeks rather than once every 3 weeks for 6 months (the total duration of chemotherapy I needed). Again, it just seemed logical to me especially since I had two kids under the age of five. Those four weeks were horrible, but I was now on a mission. I continued with the remaining five months of chemo, all the while taking my girls to their school and activities. To this day they don't remember me being ill. I needed them to see me as a fighter.

After healing, I needed to find something that gave me peace and fulfillment. I decided to go back to school to become an esthetician (a skincare therapist) and open a spa. My husband was not on board at all, but I decided that I was okay with him "not being on board" and arranged for care in the evening hours for my girls and paid my way through a one-year night-school program (thank goodness mom suggested I keep some of my money separate – that made it possible for me to take empowered action without anyone's approval.) Fast-forward one year, and I opened my spa in my local town and rocked it. I was instantly successful, in a place where no one thought I could be successful with a high-end skincare business. One day something magical happened, I was casually introduced to energy healing, something called Reiki. I had no idea what it was, but again it was that nagging feeling that I needed to follow through. I already had clients on the table for skincare, why not add some Reiki to their session?

Needless to say, it was a resounding success and something clearly brought to me by Source. As I made more and more choices to embrace my power, the Universe started sending me vibrational matches in terms of clients, resources, and opportunities that resonated to empowerment and abundance. Reiki was clearly the opportunity to take my life in a direction I had never once considered. More and more people came to me for Reiki. Then they wanted me to teach what I knew. It was clear in a few years that I needed to move out of skincare and into energy work full time, but could I really do this? Could I make a living doing energy work? I secretly loved all things spiritual but never dared to come entirely out of the closet about it!

Finally, I took that leap of faith (keep this in mind, as it's required for manifesting!) and jumped full time into energy healing. It is then that I discovered past lives. Yes, I began to intuitively sense that most people who were coming to me for energy healing had their issues rooted in a past life. So I then took another leap of faith and started researching past lives. Here I came upon the term Akashic Record, a fifth-dimensional "database" that stores all the soul information. I knew this was my next move so I sought out mentorship and learned from some of the best in the field. This is now what I do full time, making more money than I ever thought I could.

I am truly leading my soul-driven life! I finally allowed my natural intuition and healing abilities to come out in ways I never considered. Source knew all along, and kept giving me people, situations, and opportunities until I finally chose them!

I took one final empowered action and ended the nearly 20 year marriage that brought me so much unhappiness. I bought a brand new house I paid for with cash and moved myself and my girls there. This man and I were just not a good fit for one another, but I thanked him for helping me discover my own empowerment. I had lots of difficult choices to make along my journey, something we all have to do in order to embrace our personal power. This is now my mission to teach as many people as I can of their own ability to create the life of their dreams by embracing their personal power and lead a soul-driven life.

What is personal power? To make decisions for yourself based on self-love, and honoring what brings you happiness. It is knowing that if you make a mistake you can course-correct and figure it out. It is the constant pursuit of joy and choosing it over anything or anyone, and knowing that Source will deliver exactly what you need along the way. It doesn't matter who you are, what your situation is, or how far you think you need to go to reach your goal. You have everything you need to get there by living your soul gifts without hesitation, and clearing your negative repeating patterns through new empowered action. Learning to use your Akashic Record for this process will have you changing your life by leaps and bounds, much faster than you could ever imagine! Reach out, I'd love to mentor you through your karma and into your soul-powered joy and abundance!

PATTY OLIVER

Patty has provided transformational energy healing sessions for the past 12 years, with clients all around the world. Spiritual leaders, authors, healers, political activists, entrepreneurs and more regularly seek her healing and spiritual guidance. Patty is an Akashic Records Master Practitioner, Reiki Master, Channel, Intuitive Energy Healer, spiritual teacher and international best-selling author. Her healing sessions are divinely guided by your spirit guides, archangels and ascended masters to clear karmic patterns in your Akashic Record, balance your chakras and auras and help you align to your divine soul blueprint to manifest your highest potential. Patty also offers online courses in Akashic Records and energy healing, whether you are an individual seeking knowledge or a healing practitioner wanting to expand your practice. She is located in Portland, Oregon and conducts her Akashic Readings by Zoom to anyone in the world. You can schedule Readings directly on her website, and you can connect with Patty in any of the following ways:

Email: patty@pattyoliver.com
Web: www.pattyoliver.com
Instagram:
www.instagram.com/pattyoliverenergyhealer
Facebook:
www.facebook.com/pattyoliverenergyhealer

2

ROSALIE DEHMUIR

PEACE NOTES FOR THE SOUL

MY LIFE AND SPIRITUAL JOURNEY

*W*hen I first sat down to write about my spiritual journey, I was urged to start from the time I was three years old. However, I soon realised here too was the starting point of my life story. I can't separate them. They go hand in hand all the way, intertwined, just as our physical body and our emotions are connected.

My first memory is as a little girl, living in a house with my parents and a friend of theirs who was boarding with us. Mum and Dad regularly asked him to look after me when they went out. I just couldn't understand why they would do that because I was being sexually abused. How were they not aware of what was happening? Every time they started to get themselves ready to go out, I would be physically sick. Surely, they should've understood, but instead, I would be in trouble. They thought I was just trying to get attention.

I wanted so much to tell them not to go. I wanted to share what was happening, but I couldn't. This man threatened to hurt my parents if

I told them. Instead, I had to endure what he did to me. This happened over two years.

I finally felt saved when my parents, my new brother and I were transferred to start a new life in New Guinea. Arriving in Port Moresby was a breath of fresh air to me. It was such a different life, so natural and friendly, especially the native boys. One night not long after we arrived, a group came to welcome us by beating their drums. Standing in the bottom of our garden, I just had to go and ask them why they were doing it. The boys said that they worship the Sun God, pointing above my head. Being quite small at the time, I was very puzzled and asked where again? They continued to point closer to my head. I still did not understand so nodded to be polite and waved them goodbye and went inside to tell my father.

My father laughed when I told him, and he said "Ra is the Sun God, but I don't think he is here on top of your head he laughed" however the boys kept up the regular drumming performances until we left when I was ten years of age.

The next place we visited was Egypt. WOW, I was so happy to visit the Pyramids. I felt like I had come home. In those days, I could stand really close as there were no barricades to stop me. The energy coming from them was so warm and intense it made my heart race with excitement. Once again, my father thought I was crazy because he couldn't understand why I wasn't writing notes for school, like all the other kids. Instead, I was hugging Pyramids.

It was there that I heard the first voice, a male voice saying "Welcome". I looked around us and couldn't see anybody except my father, who was now busy looking at facts about the pyramids? I kept this to myself with a secret grin, I felt they were guardian angels looking after us. I really loved everything about Egypt and was determined to research everything I could because I did not understand what I was feeling. I was a ten-year-old girl who was more at home in Egypt than anywhere else I had been.

I would go right up to the pyramids and wrap my arms around as best I could. The energy coming from them was so strong, it would buzz right through my body. I had never felt like that before. One day the male voice told me "You are home". Again, I felt the sense that it was a guardian angel. I felt that it was the voice of Ra.

The next stop on our world trip was Venus, Italy. This was another "aha" moment for me. We were searching for a coffee place, which seemed to be scarce. After our long plane flight, we thought it might be nice to find a local cafe instead of the big one at our hotel. I had a sudden brainwave and told Dad that just around the next corner, upstairs there was an extremely popular cafe. He looked at me and laughed but decided to show me how wrong I could be. To his shock when we walked into the shop of curios, the shopkeeper said:" I am sorry Senior, not now but 100 years ago, upstairs there was an incredibly famous cafe with food and dancing. How did you know this?" Dad looked stunned and shook his head, I smiled and said, "I really don't know how I know". The lady smiled, and we went on to find another with Dad then calling me "Wendy the Witch". It made me laugh.

The next part of my journey was simply growing up. I had arrived as a little girl in America and met others my age. It was then that I realised I was quite different. I had been living on an island until then. I was introduced to being a young woman with the trimmings of knowing how to do my hair and make my face up, it was quite a transformation.

Returning to our home in Sydney, Australia was a huge wake-up call to me. My parents had kept the home in the suburbs from when Dad was transferred to New Guinea. I knew from movies that in America it was noticeably big and fast, however as we arrived home, I was shocked by how people were running in the streets. I thought there must be a fire somewhere. Mum explained they are always like this in the city. I had been used to island living where nobody rushes. It's amazing how quickly you soon fall into the trap of walking just as fast.

At 13 I started high school and was hairdressing part-time after school. This is when I started to feel messages. I felt I needed to tell the clients, but I was nervous about this as it was so new to me. So, when I received a few, I asked some if they minded me telling them with no guarantee it would be right. It was a practice. They did not mind at all and each one said the message was what they needed, and they were always grateful for the messages. So, I continued.

I was a happy teenager for quite a while until I was betrayed by a friend at a party. The young boys had decided to put vodka in the punch, and I passed out and when I awoke, I came to be raped by a boy who I had considered a friend. I was devastated by this as I thought I had left this treatment behind me. It brought horrible memories back from my childhood, not that they were the same, but I was being abused all over again. I just could not tell my parents again, I felt so much anger and so much shame.

I was so angry with the boy for what he did and didn't want to see him again. Then I found out that I was pregnant. When I told him, he immediately said to abort it so nobody would know. I was horrified as I had always wanted children. I thought about telling my parents then, but before I could, the police came to the door to tell my father they had caught the boy stealing money so could pay for an abortion for me. OMG! My father screamed at me to go to my room, and he would talk to me.

When I told my parents what happened they had him charged with rape. My mother wanted me to go away on a farm somewhere to have it and adopt it out, however the following week I came down with German Measles. The doctor said I could not carry the child as it may be deformed or disabled in some way. This is difficult for anyone to face, let alone a 15-year-old. It was decided that I had to go to the hospital to have it aborted. This was such an unhappy time, and I became very ill. I ended up with blood poisoning so severe that I was at the point of passing over. The doctors had a hard time bringing me back, I know because I remember me thinking "I am not sure if I want to come back if this keeps happening to me", then suddenly a voice with a warm tone said, "Yes you are going Back" and then "you have a mission". Then I remember being back. Secretly I hoped that all that had happened hadn't spoiled my chance at having more children because I loved children so much.

At around the same age, I took an interest in palmistry and did a lot of reading about it. I started to study palms and found them to be fascinating. While I was looking at them, they spoke to me, not just the facts about what each line meant but I just knew what they said. I was always looking at palms. One lady, who lived interstate, used to come every year to get her hair done while she was on vacation. She always wanted me to do a reading for her. One time, she said she would not have her palm read unless I would take some money for it, as I had never done so before. She said to me I should learn to balance how I give and receive energies. A good lesson for us all I now know, to place value on ourselves.

When I was 19, I fell down a concrete stair on my tailbone while I was cutting hair. I had a concussion and a painful spine, but the damage didn't come out for a while. I had no feeling in my legs and ended up having smashed discs. I had to have surgery. During the surgery, I again passed over. This time I experienced the most beautiful colours and heard a voice that said, "not this time". This landed me in a wheelchair for two years before I fought my way out with every bit of determination I could gather up.

My spiritual journey then had a quiet spell for a few years. I got married, bought a hairdressing salon, and became a businesswoman, and eventually, I finally fell pregnant. This was the absolute joy of my life, however, at four months gestation I had to be hospitalised until I had my baby because I kept having blood clots (DVTs) in my legs. When she was born, yes it was a girl, who I knew I was having, the clots were going to my lungs, so I had to have surgery. My baby had to stay with me in hospital for the first three months so I could feed her and bond with her. I was in and out of hospital for the next three years with clotting issues. My mother helped by looking after the baby and would bring her in at visiting times, which was an awfully hard time for us all, Mum was wonderful because I had three lung surgeries over the next three years.

Therefore, when I would come home, I had to take time out of everything, except my own healing, and to spend as much time really getting to know my daughter. This was the best part of my healing journey. I also moved interstate by the doctor's orders to a warmer climate so my blood would not clot so easily.

Living in Queensland did make my life better, and I healed a lot quicker. I fought every day to be well again, and I was happy to be reunited with my daughter and living a more normal life. It wasn't long before she was off to school, and I was back to work at hairdressing. My spiritual journey was coming back to me gradually, with messages for my clients and the strong feelings of presence and protection had returned.

I joined a creative dance class for exercise, and fun which was good for me and my body. I did this for a while until one night a car ran me off the road and attacked me. They couldn't get me fully out of the car, however four people, three men and a woman, had my upper body pulled out. They were choking me and beating me until I somehow put my foot down and escaped to home where I was speechless. The police came and tried to find them, but I do not know if they ever caught them. I could not talk properly for a while and was in shock, I just could not believe this had happened to me. I had to spend the night in the hospital for observation. Physically I was very bruised, but emotionally I was more than bruised. This was just too much! It triggered me to have a nervous breakdown.

I hit the bottom of the pit, I felt as if I was in this life to be abused, I wanted out, the only thing that kept me alive, was my daughter.

This was the last time I was abused in my life. The reason I have shared these as part of my spiritual journey and my life is because there has been a pattern of abuse. This is easily seen now, but I did not realise it at the time because I didn't deal with the abuse when I was three. I held it inside of me and made the pattern repeat over and over, whether it was physical or emotional, or both.

The solution is to forgive the person who has wronged you, abused you, hurt you. There is no need to do this to their face, just within yourself, from your heart. Forgiveness doesn't mean condoning their behaviour. This is for your sake only so you may be free to move forward in your life without repeating the same pattern.

Now moving forward, I was a single parent currently. After two failed marriages, I was getting used to being on my own. My daughter was 17 years old and had decided to live with her father. I was going to dance classes to keep fit and have fun, my health seemed to be a lot better if I didn't overdo it.

I had been going out on a few dates, which never ended well. So, I decided to have a serious talk with my guides, who I trusted. I meditated and asked, "please either send me my Twin Flame who is perfect for me. Or if I am meant to be alone for the rest of my life, then I want to know in seven days". I fell asleep in tears.

The next day it left my mind. I planned to go to the dance hall the following week as I was collecting money for a Christmas gift for the teachers. I wasn't supposed to be there that night however it turned out it was meant to be. A man came up to me to ask if he could sign up for the dance classes. I said "You have come to the wrong night, this is the graduating night, not the beginner's night" so he said then "may I stay and see what I am here to learn? "Of course," I said.

He stayed and watched me dance all night. Finally, at the end of the night, he came up to me and introduced himself. He said, "Would you please be my partner through the classes?". By this time, I had been checking him out thinking him to be a nice guy, so why not? So, I said , "yes, I would".

The following Monday, two days later (which was five days after I asked my guides), we started the new dance classes and dinner together. We have not been separated since.

Ashley proposed to me two weeks later. I accepted and we were married eight months later.

After finding forgiveness within me, and releasing and clearing the patterns of the past, my messages got a lot stronger. I started doing a lot of readings. I could not get enough spiritual knowledge and wanted to study something but did not know which way to go yet. Then I saw an ad in the paper about healing with the eyes and that really appealed to me. I just knew it was the right moment to turn my life around, no more abuse, only positive good times ahead.

I approached the people running it and joined immediately. I felt a positive connection. The course was six months of study and healing. My eyes showed how much I had been through so they knew I would be a challenge; it was but I succeeded beautifully.

In the six months, my life made an incredible turnaround. I found knowledge is powerful, it truly is. If you understand how your body and your emotions work together, you can bring them into harmony instead of fighting each other.

I thought after forgiving and healing my organs, my emotions would get off, scot-free. But no, I had a fall three years ago and broke my hip in half. I also damaged my spine to a point of being not fixable so wasn't able to walk or drive anymore.

I am an Empath and have so much love to help others come back from challenges or prevent them from going there as well. I have gained as much knowledge as I can. I am a Master/Teacher, Reiki, Seichim, Karuna, Gematria Numerology, Gestational Integration, Spiritual Iridology, Lifetimes Kinesiology, palmistry, Medium.

With all these tools and healing modalities, my accident has not stopped me from doing all the things I love. However, what does that all matter when you read my next and last paragraph?

I would like to say to anyone having a challenge that you think is impossible to come out of, please do not give up. Never ever give up, it is never too late in life to be free and to be happy. I am 74 years old. I am both free, happy, and loving each day as it comes.

This, I wish for You.

ROSALIE DEHMUIR

Rev Rosalie DehMuir is a Healer & Teacher of Usui Reiki Master, Karuna Reiki, Free Distant Healing. Master Seichim/Seckem/All Love/Teacher, Spiritual Iridologist, Lifetimes Kinesiology, Gematria (Ancient Egyptian Numerology) Teacher, Past Life Therapist, Virtual Lap band Hypnotherapist, Soul Rescue Therapist, The Journey by Brandon Bay therapist, Meditation Teacher, (Beginners & Advanced). Opening to Channel (Mediumship) Teacher, Ordained Isis High Priestess Trainer, Psychic Reader, Clairvoyant, Medium, Palmistry, Face Reader, & now Author. Spiritual Coach/ Mentor.

Rosalie loves all she does with a passion and works straight from the heart directly to your heart and has been for 30 years professionally. Most of Rosalie's work these days are online and around the globe. Ordained Goddess Isis Priestess

I believe in holistic healing and love to help a person find their true self & inner awareness & inner power to self-heal & love life.

The Crystal Gateway: www.facebook.com/roseashm
Rosalie Aka Wholistic: www.facebook.com/RMakawholistic

3

DAWN MARIE DELAHUNT

BABY'S SOUL—MOTHER TO BE—JOURNEY TO GET THERE

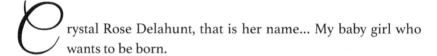

*C*rystal Rose Delahunt, that is her name... My baby girl who wants to be born.

Today I sit here, September 24, 2021, at 4:42 am as I await my 6:45 am appointment with my fertility doctor. I am happy to see it's almost 4:44 am, an ANGEL NUMBER. As I type "number" the clock strikes 4:44. I have the chills (or you may call it goosebumps), throughout my entire body!! Maybe today I will get the good news, that my uterine lining wall has grown thicker, and we can finally get my IVF transfer date!

Suddenly, I feel the presence of my baby's soul, "Crystal Rose Delahunt". I am a medium and have been connecting to my baby's soul for many years. She has been guiding me and giving me the strength to keep pushing forward to have her. She chose me to be her Mom and I am excited to bring her here into the physical world.

"Who is there?" I ask.

"Mommy it's me ...."

"Crystal?"

"Yes... Mommy, it's me..."

"Hello, my beautiful baby girl..."

"Thank you so much for your strength and determination... I am Coming!!!"

"I know you are. I can't wait to get pregnant, hold the pregnancy, and deliver you. I can't wait to start our beautiful family. You are going to be such a great addition to The Delahunt Family"

"Yes, I know you can't wait, but the timing has to be just right for you, for me and the Universe. I know you don't understand or know why right now but you will. I sit here with many baby souls that want to be born. On February 28th, 2020, I know your heart was broken, when you found out my heart stopped beating when you were 4 months pregnant with me. Yes, it was me and thanks for trusting and knowing it was me all along. As I told you that day, I am still coming and to let you know that you will be a stand for so many women that have the desire to get pregnant, that yearn to be a mother. You will be a stand to tell them to keep going no matter what!! Thank you for answering your call... Yes, Mommy, this is part of your soul purpose just as you thought."

"Crystal, I thought my purpose was to awaken people to their gifts. To awaken and inspire all to see with their "Angel Eyes".

"Yes, Mommy it is, but there is more. As you grow, you ascend here on Earth and truly do the work as you have, you get more and more to do as a lightworker, or as Robert Scarpa mentions, Light Bringer. That is what you are, and what you are here to bring; the Light."

(I suddenly feel the chills all through me as I type that last word... *"Light".*)

I know the world needs more light. I know I am supposed to shine my light within and be a role model. Sometimes, it's hard and I feel sad and defeated, but I always try to pick myself up and keep pushing forward. There is always something inside of me keeping me going. There is more to life than the mundane waking up, going to work, and paying the bills. We all have a purpose... *"We Are All Special and We Are All Gifted."* We are here today, right now, to recognize and find our purpose and live a life on purpose.

That is what I am here to do today, to share my fertility journey at the age of 51. It's never too late, and you're never too old, to reach the dreams that are in your heart.

Let's start at the beginning... Crystal has always been my favorite girl's name; I never knew why until now.

It's now 5:04, let's check the Angel number.

"Your angels are with you, guiding you to cultivate what's important and let go of what's not." [1]

Wow, how perfect, I know I do too much, and I must have better habits, self-care, meditation, and exercise. Why don't I make time for myself?

Now it is 5:07. What is that Angel Message, I wonder?

"You are being guided to make room for miracles. Miracles manifest when you make room for them."

How perfect, the perfect two messages for me, as I am awaiting the miracle of pregnancy right now for Crystal Rose Delahunt to be born. This brings a smile to my face. It's going to happen, I just know it. I recently taught a class on manifesting miracles using the Law of Attraction, vision boards, prayer, and meditation to bring your dreams to fruition.   As I type these words now, a moth sits on my screen where my Reiki Healing Radio Station of Pandora is on. Yes, I need more silence in my life, more meditation. I must take care of myself to be ready for Crystal to come.

Now, I feel guided to draw an Angel Card for the day, for this moment. I pause to say my prayers and set my intention for a message.

I began with a beautiful prayer by one of my mentors Reverend Elaine Thomas, Fellowship of the Spirit, Lily Dale, NY.

"Oh God as we open the door to communication, in the Unity of the Holy Spirit the Great I am Presence, for we give thanks, for we know that the words spoken (and the healing received) are filled with your Love, Truth, Wisdom and Understanding." Amen.

This is the prayer I use to start every prayer, meditation, and channeling session. As I say my prayers, I always bring in the White Light of God and the Angels within and around me. I also bring in Mother Earth energy up through me, surrounding me with healing energy to ground and center me.

As I type, I am drawn to the clock again, it's 5:20. Let's see what the Angel message is.

"Have Faith in God to help you change your life for the better. Miracles can rapidly transform situations, so expect them to occur!"

I love it! Expect Miracles... I received this message for a reason... MIRACLES!

Here is another Angel number message for 520 which is just as amazing.

"Your connection with God is stronger than ever. Welcome home to love."

Now let's center, ground and pray. as I select a card for the day... CHILLS!!! Yes, the magic happened again...

The first card I see is a card that was flipped up, it reads *"Forgiveness"*. *"Your emotions are healing, which enables you to open to a greater love. I will help you release anger and unforgiveness from your heart and mind."* This card is perfect. I am hard on myself for not doing enough, for not being enough, but I am enough, I have been through a lot, and I am at the right time right now. All is well.

The next card I chose is *"Take action"*. This is very powerful. We must be in Action to allow the Law of Attraction to work for us... "God helps those who help themselves". We don't just put pictures on a board and wait for it to happen, we must be an active participant in our life, we get to ASK for what we want, we are blessed to invite God and the Angels into our lives, and most importantly to BELIEVE with unwavering faith that it's going to happen. That has been said to be the biggest secret to manifesting. "BELIEVE", then be open to RECEIVE. "ASK, BELIEVE and RECEIVE." This is what many authors state as the Law of Attraction, but one important step is missing "TO BE IN ACTION", we must be in ACTION. "Action is the fundamental key to success". For me, it's following my guidance to go to a fertility clinic and realize that with modern medicine, miracles are possible.

Then as I continue to shuffle, a card jumps out...

"I am the Angel Of families. A happy change or addition is coming to your family." There is a picture of an angel holding a baby. This makes my heart sing.

Crystal is coming, I love the signs, the messages, for this is what keeps me going on this fertility journey. Boy, it has been a long one. As I prepare for my appointment, I go with hope and faith for this next step.

What an appointment it was. It's happening. My body is ready, and I have my IVF transfer date. All the signs are there, next Thursday, September 30th will be the date that I will get pregnant!! Crystal is ready to come.

I am so happy to have received this news, now I get to prepare myself with the appropriate medications for my body to accept and hold the pregnancy. I am so excited!! This is happening!!

"Mommy, thank you for being patient. I know it's been a long time coming, but the time is now. I am ready and The Universe is ready for us both to begin this next phase, it's our destiny."

This journey has been a long road. On October 12th, 2013, at 10 am. I married Clement Francis Delahunt III. He has a strong and beautiful name. To me, it sounds like royalty. I finally found and married my prince at the age of 42. I will never forget one beautiful night on our honeymoon in Cancun, Mexico. As part of our beautiful, romantic dinner, the hotel at which we were staying asked if we'd like to help release baby turtles. As we released them, we both said a prayer to the ocean. We said, "Here is to our twins, Crystal and Clem." It was at that moment that our fertility journey truly began.

We've had some roadblocks and challenges and tackled them one at a time. Over time, my dream of having children never went away but for some reason, we seemed to have gotten off track. I started to lose myself. I gained weight, I was drinking too much alcohol. I was just not happy. I was blessed with three beautiful stepchildren, which I fully embraced into my heart and accepted and loved as my own, as I still do today. But the burning desire to have children was still there and was strong.

I was connecting with Crystal, the soul of my baby girl through automatic writing, and she even came through my students and colleagues. The messages were clear and strong. She was with me and wanted to be born.

I truly believe we all have the ability to connect with our Spirit Guides, Angels and Loved Ones. Life exists before birth and after death. I came to this belief after my spiritual awakening, post the tragic events of September 11th, 2001. I felt the pain of the world and had lost my friend, a fireman named Michael J Cawley. After that day, I started having spiritual experiences and I began my spiritual journey. I felt the pain and sadness of the world and I needed to know more. "What happened to all those souls? Where do they go? What happens next?" I was on a journey of self-discovery, as I am, still to this day. The journey of the soul is truly amazing.

I began my journey of self-discovery, or I should say "soul" discovery. I have always been drawn to psychics and mediums. One day after

9/11, I went to see Jeffrey Wands, a well-known medium in Port Washington, New York. He told me Mike was with me, he said things that there was no way he could have known. He also told me I was very sensitive and could be doing what he is doing. I was very surprised. He gave me a card for Pat Longo, a Spiritual Healer and Teacher, and this is where my spiritual journey began. I started going to Pat for private healing sessions and weekly classes. It was nice to meet so many other like-minded people. I then realized why I have always loved Angels since a young age. I started channeling messages from God, Angels, and my Loved Ones, through automatic writing. It was amazing. Since I am not a big reader, I started going to events by well-known spiritual authors. I could not get enough and loved every bit of it. Each day seemed divinely guided and synchronistic. I learned about Energy Healing called "Reiki", which truly helped me heal and get past challenges in my life. I had a deep desire to learn and study more. I became a Reiki Master Teacher, Angel Card Reader and an Ordained Minister. I then started my business Angel Eyes Dawn Marie, with my tag line "Let Me Help You See Your Inner Truth."

During my readings, although there would be a specific message for them from their Angels and Loved Ones coming through, there was always a common theme. "You can do this too." Spirit was always telling me that they can connect with their Angels and Loved Ones too. We all have this ability. I always seemed to be letting them know they can do this themselves in the readings, which led me to become a Spiritual Teacher.

I began to teach an intuitive development course with my Reiki Master Teacher, Lorraine Austin and it felt so good to teach. The course was called ADT, "Awaken, Develop and Trust Your Intuitive Ability" It was so amazing to see our students open and connect. It was purely magical!

As the years went on, I continued to work full time in the financial world and would do readings, teach, and study during nights and weekends. I volunteered and worked fairs throughout Long Island for organizations such as Eyes of Learning and Long Island Reiki Association. I loved being able to help people, to bring them hope and healing during their time of need. In July 2012, I became part of the Long Island Healing Arts and Learning Center, which I am still a part of today, alongside the owners, Laura Maglio and Theresa Sarin. Their vision is to help support Lightworkers on their journey.

"We are called as lightworkers, peacemakers and healers to use our tools at this time to help bring harmony and peace to our earth and all its kingdoms. Our compassion, light and love are greatly needed now to bring healing to all who are suffering and frightened. Let us gather energetically to assist humanity and our earth. Please continue to hold the Light."

-Theresa Sarin

I became the primary intuitive development teacher at the center, teaching students to connect to their intuition using angel cards, automatic writing, mediation, mediumship and challenging. I am still doing this today, as I am also expanding beyond my local market, to a national and international client base with an online platform called ZOOM.

During this time, Crystal's presence was always strong, to me. It's now been nearly ten years since I started this journey in 2012. All the emotional ups and downs bring me to where I am today.

I found my current fertility doctor in the Summer of 2019. I met wonderful people through his practice and started the process of IVF. My doctor then changed practices, but I stayed loyal to him as I knew he was my doctor, and I will get pregnant. Sure enough, on October 22, 2020 I received my embryo transfer and later found out I was pregnant. Hearing that news was a magical, beautiful moment. I enjoyed every doctor appointment and hearing my baby's heartbeat. It was a dream come true. At the 8-week mark, I sent out for a test to see if it was a boy or girl, for in my heart I knew it was Crystal. Sure enough, the test results came in and it was a girl. I was overjoyed!! We got to share the news during the holiday season. Then on January 28, 2021, I went for my four month sonogram and there was no heartbeat. I was beyond devastated. We were devastated. My husband held me and said, "Don't worry we will keep trying". I've never felt so much pain, I was in denial. I told the doctor to check again as this can't be. Why would I be guided and led to this point? We had just shared with family and friends at three months that we were pregnant. I even went live on social media to share the news. This can't be happening. When I got home after receiving the news, I felt Crystal's presence and heard her little voice, all cheery and joyful, but I was devastated...

"Mommy, Mommy, Mommy!! it's ok, I am still coming, it is supposed to be this way. There are so many baby souls that need to be born and your story, your journey will help give their Mommies and Daddies strength. It's ok Mommy."

She made me smile, she gave me hope that I will get through this. I felt a sudden sense of calm and peace, that my dream is not over, and this loss is for a greater purpose... to bring strength to older women in their 40-50's. Strength, Determination and Resilience....to let them know is never too late. With modern medical miracles and a whole lot of faith, it's possible. These souls want to be born, and even though the journey may be long and challenging, it is possible. I am Strong!! I have unwavering faith that Crystal is coming.

Since my loss, it has been a long year of healing and testing. There have been emotional ups and downs, and many delays. I stand in front of you right now, today with complete and total faith I will be pregnant. She is here with me now to share with the world, no matter what challenges come our way, we keep going, we never quit. If you keep believing in the dream, it will come true.

Today, September 25th, 2021, I begin the progesterone injections to prepare my body for my IVF transfer five days later. I am so excited to finally be at this next step. I have been waiting for this since I lost the baby on January 28, 2021. I know I will be pregnant, hold the pregnancy and have my beautiful baby girl. The time is right now.

The transfer date has come; September 30th between 1:00-2:00 pm, the embryo of my healthy baby girl has been successfully transferred. Yes, it's a girl, with genetic testing they can test the health and sex of the baby. Now I await the next doctor visit to get the official news that I am in fact pregnant!!!

Time has gone by, and I now have the news that I have been waiting for. I went to the doctors to take my pregnancy blood test and the results are in. I am NOT pregnant. How could this be? Why am I being delayed again? What went wrong? Is it my fault? I thought now is the time!! I don't understand!!

Feeling Crystal's presence

"Mommy now is the time, we are one step closer. As I mentioned, timing has to be just right for you, for me and the Universe. You're right on track for me to come, again you are now another step closer to me coming. I am STILL coming!!"

"Why did you lead me to believe I was going to get pregnant on my last transfer date?

"Mommy, sometimes we need to lead you to the next step even if the outcome is not as it's intended to be, but you need to go through it no matter what, lessons need to be learned. If you knew the outcome, you may skip a step, and every step leads you to the next one. Also, sometimes it's just out of our control when dealing with science and spirituality. Please Mommy, just have faith and know all the stars will align and it will happen"

Chills!!

Suddenly I feel a sense of peace after days of sadness with this news. She is still coming and I will be pregnant soon when the time is right.

I SURRENDER!! I know I cannot control it. I just must show up every step of the way, and continue to follow my spiritual guidance. I know I will get there. I have faith and know I will be pregnant!! I will never, ever give up!!

My purpose has evolved to not only awaken people to their gifts but to let all women know it's never too late, to never give up on their dream of being a mom.

Always believe in your dreams, you are never too young or too old. Believe in the Magic of The Universe, believe in the Power of Prayer and Manifest Miracles in your life. You are worth it. *"We Are All Special and We Are All Gifted"*. Your life is what you create, so create the life you want.

I feel guided to draw one more card, and of course, it is perfect, "MANIFESTING POWER". This is a validation that you too can have the life of your dreams, anything at all you desire, including the baby you want, follow your heart, and live your life "ON" purpose. This card states *"Use your spiritual gifts and natural abilities to attract your desired outcome."*

I will continue to use my gifts. I will continue to connect with my baby's soul, " Crystal". For I am a mother to be and this is my journey to get there. My soul connection to Crystal keeps me going. She will guide me every step of the way, for there are no disappointments, only steps closer to giving birth to her. I have complete unwavering faith that she is still coming!!

Time is Now!! Time is now for us all to have the life we desire and dream about and so it is!! Namaste!!

---

1. Angel Numbers - Kyle Gray

DAWN MARIE DELAHUNT

Dawn Marie Delahunt aka "Angel Eyes Dawn Marie," is an Angelic Oracle, Psychic Medium, Spiritual Teacher, and Intuitive Development Coach. Dawn's signature gift is that she has a unique ability to inspire and awaken the innate intuitive gifts of others. Dawn does this through her readings, certification courses, workshops, and intuitive development classes.

After losing a friend in the tragic 9/11 events, Dawn had an awakening. She learned that by creating her own spiritual practices, connecting with Spirit, and using energetic protocols on a regular basis, that she could transform her pain into her power.

Dawn encourages her clients and those in her free monthly online sessions to rise above and see the love so that they can live a peaceful, happier, more fulfilled life.

"Be the you, you are meant to be...Let me help you see your inner truth. And know...We are all Special, We are all Gifted."

Connect with Dawn
Website: www.angeleyesdawnmarie.com
Facebook: www.facebook.com/angeleyesdawnmarie
Instagram: www.instagram.com/angeleyesdawnmarie

4

THERESA COLE

PERSEVERANCE THROUGH PAIN

A chilly morning in February of 1985 started not too different than any other day. I was rushing around getting ready for school and having the nonsensical issues getting motivated to get up so early so that I could drag myself to church as I did every morning. So, there I was, sliding into church a few minutes late and inevitably needing to leave my backpack in the back of the church, which was the norm when we came to church late. Annoyed, I quietly found my seat and settled into mass, sitting on the left-hand side of the church toward the middle. As I sat bored and my mind wandered a million different places, I drew my attention to a man I had never seen before. He seemed out of place, but maybe he was there with the music teacher. As each row got up and received communion, my stomach started to hurt, and I felt uneasy. This was not a feeling I ever had in church. After I received Holy Eucharist, I started back to my seat, walking down the side aisle. I glanced up from my reverent stance; we locked eyes. So sick, I am going to puke! Feeling scared, with full-bodied chills, I wanted to run! I wanted to hide! Anything to get out of there. He looks soulless! So creepy looking! What was in the case sitting next to him in the pew?

The relief fell over me when mass ended and chatting with classmates distracted me from the awful feeling in my stomach. As I was being ushered out of the church, I found myself engaging in conversation with friends while walking into school. Approaching my classroom, I realized I forgot my backpack in church. Hurry, you better get it and be back by the time the bell rings, I thought to myself. There is that feeling again; sick and dizzy. Why am I scared to open the door? Racing thoughts spun in my head. Maybe I can get it later. Oh, come on, stop being so weird, I said to myself. Opening the big door, even heavier than before, I bent over to grab my stuff quickly. Something made me lean to the left, looking down the middle aisle of the church, all the way to the alter. Oh God, oh God, get out of here; the man, our priest, why, what is the man pointing at Father? Is that a gun? No, it is not! I must get out of here. Running back to school, I heard a loud BANG come from church. Running faster than ever before, dizzy and feeling ill, I made it back to my desk.

Desperately trying to make sense of what I witnessed, I realized that class had not yet started, even well after the bell rang. Paper airplanes flying, and my classmates had begun to talk over each other, but I grew even more anxious. Finally, our teacher entered the classroom, which had seemed like an eternity. She was so sad, with tears in her eyes, and asked us all to sit down and be quiet. Then the words came out of her mouth, words I already knew she was going to say. Our beloved priest, the man that we all thought the world of, had been murdered. That was not it; two others had also been shot and murdered in the church. Oh my God! It was true, and I already knew to some degree what had happened. I already knew.

Since I can remember, even as a toddler, I had always had a way of visualizing whatever somebody was saying to me. It was almost as if I could put myself in that place, time, and situation. Feeling every emotion, understanding thoughts, and knowing the outcome, was not unusual for me during this time in my life. To me, this was normal, and to some degree, no different than any other child, recalling my family telling me I had a wild imagination. Unfortunately, and through no fault of their own, this left me feeling dismissed, misunderstood, and of course, invalidated. I had "imaginary" friends, my family often told me, but they were not "imaginary"; the spirits were real to me. Usually, I was awoken by a spiritual presence, and it was terrifying. When I was ten, my father tried his best to console me in the middle of the night as I screamed and shook, hiding my head under the covers. It was almost as if he understood me or could have possibly had similar experiences because he listened and knew what to say. That was the most comforting thing. My dad was my hero, my place of solace! Finally, somebody understood me, and I was no longer alone on my "deserted island."

Then, I was connected to things I did not understand and had abilities that I could not identify, but I accepted it. After that tragic day in February, life as I knew it changed so much; sadness, grief, and darkness filled my heart. We all forced ourselves to go about our day-to-day activities, sporting events, and life in general. Child psychologists and teachers worked with all of us during the days, weeks, and months following the shooting. The church was cleaned of the bloodstains and blessed, cleansed, and cleared of all negative energy by the highest priests, bishops, and cardinals, all to make it a safe and positive environment for students, teachers, and parishioners. Yet, in my mind, I never stopped seeing the man with the gun to Father's head or the dead stare in his eyes. They wiped away the physical evidence of the tragedy, but it was never going to be gone in my mind and my body. Trauma resided deep inside the cells of my body, causing illness, disease, and emotional triggers.

As the year passed, the loneliness inside me never went away, no matter the support, love, and kindness of others around me. My ability to cope with high school drama, friend conflicts, or just the pressure of school was difficult for me. I retreated inside myself, just as I tried to stuff the memories down deep of the shooting. I felt awkward, not accepted, and did not want to be at school, but I did my best to be "normal." I felt so disconnected from myself that many decisions I made from that point were from the space of loneliness and loss. Again, I felt alone on a deserted island, struggling to keep alive and thriving, despite my family's efforts to be supportive. How could they support me when they did not understand what I needed? I did not let them in! I was closed off.

I struggled to find my voice in the years to follow. My relationship with my boyfriend, later my husband, was not healthy, as my foundation was still on very shaky, uneven ground, I longed for balance, safety, and acceptance. I felt I had found what I was longing for, and for the most part, I did. However, I would have done anything to keep this relationship from falling apart and was terrible at setting boundaries, having a voice, and being confident and strong. I was vulnerable! Oh, I wish it were different back then, but it was a trauma effect in how I coped with the relationship. I became the fixer, running circles around him, ensuring his happiness when I was screaming on the inside. I was good at fixing everything, calming the waters. The co-dependency of our relationship was a cycle that was too difficult and painful to walk away. I needed him for security, and he needed me for his happiness, at whatever cost. And, however, messed up as it was, it was my reality. I lost myself.

An immense joy, the first I had experienced in a long time, was the birth of my first child, a girl. She was perfect in every way, and my heart filled with so much happiness, I could not contain it. This feeling inside me was something I had not felt in years, a welcomed newfound joy in my life. I loved being a new mom, not to say it was not challenging at first, but we got through the post-partum depression, and life was contentment. She was a good, contented baby. Those first few months were happy with memorable moments, baby talk, poopy diapers, and quiet nights watching her sleep and grow. Those precious moments, wondering if she were having sweet dreams and knowing that I would do anything to make her life as beautiful as she was. My heart was whole again!

Working at the clinic, checking people in for their appointments was a job I enjoyed. It was another busy day at work as I was anxiously awaiting my mom and dad's visit after my dad's doctor appointment. I loved my visits with my dad. He was always so grounding for me, gentle and kind, and my safe place. However, that day I was uneasy and felt sick to my stomach. This feeling was unshakable, and it bothered me. I looked up from my desk, and there was my dad standing before me with tears in his eyes. Oh, God! This isn't good, I thought to myself. My head was spinning, feeling sick to my stomach, and now shaking. "I have leukemia," he said. Looking over my dad's right shoulder, my mom was standing there with so much sadness and fear in her eyes, I knew it was terrible news. What do I do? What do I say? Now I need to be the gentle soul for my dad. The only words I could come up with were, "it's going to be okay," as I put my hand on his. Who the hell was I kidding? Is that all you have? I asked myself. He continued to explain that his prognosis was grim and needed to start chemotherapy immediately. And so began the beginning of the end.

My dad was the most loving, patient, kind, and compassionate soul I had ever known. Dad fought a painfully courageous battle with Acute Myeloblastic Leukemia (AML). Those were some gut-wrenching months. After he nearly died from the aggressive chemotherapy, he could finally rest and have quality time with his family. Unfortunately, his remission was short-lived, and he decided against additional aggressive chemotherapy. He wanted quality of life, so as a family, we honored his wishes. We kept his wishes for the father and husband he was.

On July 8, 1994, my mom, sisters, aunt (my dad's baby sister) and I, sat in the hospital at my dad's bedside. I lay there on a cot at the foot of his bed, trying to rest, eyes closed. Then, I heard a voice saying, "it's time." I sprung up and looked at my family as if asking them to explain what they said. As my eyes turned to my dad, I knew what that voice was saying. The slight color my dad had left in his gaunt face turned from pale to gray. It was time for my dad to be with God and his angels. I know he had a lot of them. We all sat in prayer, and as I bowed my head, I said to myself, please let his pain stop. Please take him to a place where he will not have to suffer anymore, and as we all laid our hands on my dad and told him it was okay to let go, he took his last breath at 3:00 am on that early morning hour of July 1994.

The loss I felt was so deep, so intense, it consumed me, and the grief stayed with me for many years to come. Desperately seeking answers to something final, death was final, or was it? I knew that my dad was still with me, I could feel him near, but I could not see him. If I tried hard, maybe I could make him appear. I wanted more time, another hug, more advice, and prayed to him. Every day I sought to persevere through my grief, loss, and trauma, and so I began to dig deep within to understand on a spiritual level.

Suffering from chronic illness, respiratory issues, and fatigue, I fought hard to live life the way my dad would want me to live; healthy, productive, and happy. He appeared in my dreams, so natural that I thought he was with me in the flesh, present, alive just as he always was. He said to me, "it is not time yet; you have more life to live; your kids need you." I realized that he was with me on the other side, guiding me, supporting me, and watching over all of us just as God, the angels, and spirit guides; the other side is not far. It is alongside us; we cannot see. Several months later, I woke up in the middle of the night, and dad was standing in the doorway to my bedroom with a bright, radiant light illuminating around him, wearing his typical flannel shirt and blue jeans. No words exchanged, just his big smile; peaceful and loving! Our souls would be together for all eternity!

With a renewed sense of life, I came out of the darkness and began to remember my early childhood, abilities, and connection with the spirit world. It was the connection I lost after the traumatic event at the church. Although I continued to suffer physically with chronic respiratory issues, asthma, and fatigue, I began correlating the two events in my life that had the most profound impact. Was there a connection between traumatic events and chronic illness? There was a persistent quest to understand what it all means, what I am supposed to learn, and why me? Not in the sense of feeling pity but more so feeling a calling to something greater, more in service of others. There was an innate knowing deep in my soul that it was all familiar to me.

As the years rolled by, I sought to live the best life I could. My first marriage ended in divorce, which was an exceedingly heart wrenching and challenging time for me. By this time, I had two beautiful daughters, ten years apart in age. I knew they would both have a different experience with this change; they were 14 and 4 years old. I genuinely believed in my heart and soul that this was a new beginning, free of turmoil. My heart broke for all of us, including my ex-husband. I needed to be a better person and mother, and I was determined to no longer live with sadness. And so, another life renewal began for us all.

My abilities increased even more as if to say, we hear you, we see you, we believe in you! More and more profound, I strengthened my intuition through holistic education, intuitive workshops, and a deep desire to find the missing piece. And then I discovered energy healing, and it clicked. I felt home! It resonated with me deep inside myself; the longing for what was missing was found. The glorious epiphany of my life purpose hit me like a lightning bolt. It was through my suffering, pain, and trauma that I was able to come to my life purpose – I AM A HEALER! What? Me? You see, I was born with a gift of seeing what most cannot see, feeling emotions so profoundly to the point of illness, and being connected spiritually. I suffered trauma, the death of my dad, divorce, and chronic disease so that I had no choice but to see and listen to the messages being sent directly from my spiritual family, God, angels, spirit guides, and my dad. He brought me through the darkness from the other side, just as he did in life.

Aligning to my purpose has had the most profoundly positive impact on my life. I connect with my higher self and spirit guides daily. Newly married, I have the love and support of my husband and family. I can conquer all because I have learned to find happiness within myself first. I am loved without judgment. I am speaking my truth because I am who I am. Longing for acceptance is gone and accepting myself for all that I am and all that I have gone through is freeing. Having the belief that we are all guided by the Divine light is a reality that I live every day so that I can stay on purpose and fulfill my life's journey; to be in service of others. I have been able to heal my chronic fatigue by clearing and releasing the blocked energy hiding in the dark shadows of my being. Our bodies hold trauma energetically, which can cause a myriad of symptoms, physically and emotionally. I have worked to become a clear channel for the Divine energy to flow through so that my clients can experience more joy, peace, balance, and happiness in their lives.

My philosophy of life is that experiences, good or bad, force you into becoming more of who you were meant to be; the growth realized through those experiences, we cannot honestly know ourselves. The mind, body, and soul connection show us that we are more than just our thoughts. They combine to give us identity, determine our health, and make us who we were born to be. It is our birth right!

Through life and health coaching, my goal is to provide guidance and support with a compassionate soul while challenging and empowering individuals to connect with their inner knowing so they may be able to realize their purpose and embrace the best version of themselves. The promise that I make to my clients is to hold space for them, show up authentically, actively listen, empower, and hold them accountable. I am an intuitive life coach and a compassionate guide whose talent is mentoring and connecting the world in the field of holistic healing. This story is my truth, as I live it. My life and soul's purpose are to embrace my authentic self and guide others to follow what they are called to fulfill. Choose to live the life that is calling you! CHOOSE TO LIVE IT!

THERESA COLE

Theresa Cole is a Holistic Life and Intuitive Coach specializing in energy healing, aligning clients to their life's purpose, empowering individuals by holding space, supporting, and encouraging them to honor their own truths.

Theresa's philosophy of life is that experiences, good or bad, force you into becoming more of who you were meant to be; without the growth realized through those experiences, you cannot honestly know yourself. She is a well-rounded, holistic healer with professional training in massage, Shamanism, a Certified Reiki Master, and dual certifications as a Life and Health Coach.

Theresa takes a holistically authentic approach to her coaching practices and offers services that include transformative, uniquely designed coaching programs and powerful healing sessions.

Theresa recently relocated to Southwest Florida with her husband and youngest daughter. There, she is fulfilling one of her life-long dreams, living on the Gulf Coast, soaking up the sun's energy, and enjoying the salty warm Gulf breezes.

Email: theresa.balancedcoaching@gmail.com
Website: www.inspirebalancedcoaching.com

5

DEBRA DASARO

ANGELS AND AN EMPATH

"The universe will make you so uncomfortable you will eventually have no choice."

Iyanla Vanzant

---

*a*s I sit in this very bright office room on a beautiful crisp fall October day in 2004, waiting for my boss to come in, I felt this deep sense that it was not going to be good news. She asked me early that morning to meet with her and all I heard in my head immediately was "ok....are you ready now?"

Donna walked in with her normal cheery demeanour, but after she sat down in front of me and looked me in the eyes. I knew today was going to be life-altering for me.

She proceeded to ask me a lot of questions and I could feel her dread as she reluctantly told me that I was officially "let go" from a corporate sales job that paid quite lucratively and offered me full health benefits. She also reminded me that the new company car I drove daily, which they had paid for completely (including gas), was going to be picked up in three days.

Now as a side note, I had purchased a home as a single divorced woman just two years prior. Anyone looking at me, sitting in that chair that day after being dealt tower crumbling news, would assume I would be completely and utterly devastated. She mentioned something about calling human resources, but all I could think about was "I have to go and buy a car today!"

I was in a semi-state of shock but a calming feeling was in my heart that I knew I was being propelled into a place where "my spot" was already assigned to me, the day I was born.

I walked out of the office that day without shedding a tear. Actually, relief flooded my consciousness, followed by an inner sense of peace. I smiled to myself and felt the uplifting presence of something larger than myself surround me.

For months, I knew that I did not listen to the intuitive whispers inside me that were telling me to leave this job and if I did, I would be divinely and financially supported following my divine purpose.

"She was never quite ready....but she was brave. And the Universe listens to brave."

Rebecca Ray

The fear of not having enough, not being good enough, and walking a new unknown path that most people might not understand, had stopped me. I like to now joke around when I tell this story, that the Universe whispered, then shouted and eventually had to throw bricks at me to force this change. It was quite an ego death of the identity I thought I had. It would mean shedding attachments that were not in alignment with my soul.

They gave me no choice to follow my destiny.

Destiny finds its way to you.

Sometimes you do not find yourself until life comes crashing down on you. This would be the beginning of many of those moments ....but I made a soul oath and promise to always follow my purpose to inspire and lift up as many people as I can, regardless of what happens to me.

This was the end of my life as I knew it.

I stepped into my role as a "Lightworker" that day and I never looked back.

Lightworker: Someone who devotes their life to being a bright light to the world. They bring love in the face of darkness. They are here to assist in raising the vibration of the planet. They share their authentic selves as a lighthouse in the dark.

That day I was not fully aware of even what that meant yet. I just knew one thing. The feeling of being a black sheep was far from over in my life. I knew in my heart there were many others that were "like me".

It is said that you can not live a brave life without disappointing some people. It was time to find my tribe! But first, I had to go get a car! My angels cheered as I drove that little red Grand am to the car dealership and bought a beautiful white Malibu! Red was never my color anyway!!

She talks to angels... and she is loving every moment of it.

So like a flashback in a movie, let me go back two years prior to this day. I started to finally explore my unending desire to learn more about how to tap into how to communicate with spirit guides, angels, and even loved ones that have passed on. I found it so fascinating. My own obsession to get answers was another driving force. When I say unending, I mean I just desired to soak in everything I could learn like a sponge.

"When the student is ready, the teacher appears"

Tao Te Ching

But I was soon to find out that in order to truly step into my truth I had to go so much deeper within, to shed the shadow sides of myself that were holding me back from being of the highest vibration I could be.

Just when you think you are "just fine" .....BAM! Triggers start happening like little buttons to push out trauma or unresolved issues in your body. It is like dusting off a lightbulb so more light can come through.

That's where the angels come in! Ahhhhh. Angels. They hold such a high frequency of light. They made me aware that in order to communicate with them clearly, I needed to raise my vibration so I could meet them halfway!

OK ... no problem I thought! I can meditate!

How naive I was at first!

They didn't quite mention immediately that it involved releasing the victim consciousness that my ego held onto which involved struggle, fear, lack, low self-worth and esteem, so many childhood dialogues still playing in my life.

It was dimming my light to my authentic self.

The angels are MY favorite part of my story as they have been with me since the day I was born. They are my best buddies!

They quickly guided me to start attending classes in NYC to develop my connection, to not only them but to my spirit guides and even loved ones who passed on. I could almost feel them "hurrying me along". I felt like I had wings that I just discovered!

It did not take long to validate that I had an amazing team of spiritual helpers. My Intuition was growing and my abilities to connect were getting stronger as the static cleared in my energy body.

Every class I took, I was starting to hear them speak to me in my head. I started practising giving messages and readings for others and found out this was not so foreign to me after all.

It was as if I was "remembering" who I am once again.

Little did I know that I have been feeling and hearing spirits since I was little.

Little did I know that my desire to help and heal others would begin before I was in kindergarten.

I was born in 1960, the oldest of two girls, to an Italian Mom and a Polish Dad!

I can say the food was always good, that's for sure!

But the intensity, confusion and drama were not.

Unfortunately, their marriage ended when I was 6 and there are some memories even at such a young age I remember that a child should not be subjected to. Dad had a drinking issue that would bring out a very abusive temperament towards my mother, including some that were slightly physical as well. Memories of this instilled so much fear and insecurity about my own safety in the world and were not the best first experience of what "love" is.

Despite my young age, I was so concerned about protecting my mom. I remember hugging her and consoling her with "its ok mommy...I love you" on many an occasion when she was crying uncontrollably and distraught.

My mom was reliving a cycle of the same abuse she endured and witnessed as a child. She was mentally and emotionally stuck in a codependent, victim consciousness that she never healed.

"Tell your story because your story will heal you and it will heal someone else."

Iyanla Vanzant

When we moved during the divorce, the cycle didn't stop. There were nights of chaos and fear with Dad banging on the door with threats, and wanting to have his family back together.

Underneath this horrific terror was a man that knew my mother had another man in her life now, and that escalated his addiction.

Although my Dad loved my sister and me more than anything, imagine the fear of when weekend visitations finally happened. I must say that he never touched alcohol when we were with him. But the fear of the unknown was still very very present.

The first few years, the courts only allowed Dad to take us to his parents' house. I just remember staying close to my grandmother in the kitchen, playing cards for hours or cooking. We would watch her "stories" on TV together and I would walk to ACME and go to the church down the street with her. That's where I would tell her I saw angels by the stained glass. She thought I meant artistry. "Nope, not quite grandma" I would say. She just went back to her rosary beads!

I felt so safe with her. She was strong yet loving and I felt protected with her even though she was reliant on a cane to walk.

This was all wonderful till I would be subjected to my grandfather who would come home drunk late at night and I would hear him fighting with my grandmother in polish. My grandfather was stoic and cold. The only good memory of him is the large Mr Goodbar chocolate he gave my sister and I every week.

Unfortunately, I was subjected to inappropriate behavior from him that he tried to pawn off as "loving". He passed shortly after that.

I want to express, I do have some good memories too!

Mom loved to sing and dance. I enjoyed those free happy times. She was an excellent cook too! I wish I learned more from her.

Dad, as we got older, took us on vacations and tried to be the best Dad he knew how. He never remarried and just stayed alone and looked forward to seeing his children.

My sister was always a rebel and quite outspoken. I always feared her getting hurt or worse and I tried to protect her. But chemical imbalances took over at age 15 and thus began a lifelong journey of trying to get balance in her mental wellness.

I speak up. You are not alone.

My story may be your story.

My mess is a message of HOPE.

As I got a bit older into my teen years ....I spent a lot of time in my room alone. It was totally my choice, because it was to me, the only place I could feel complete peace. I am not talking about peace just from the literal noise and chaos of the outside world which included a lot of drama within my household, but also it was a place that nobody could disturb my INNER peace.

Even then I was aware of self-protection from negativity!

I always felt I didn't belong anywhere. I always felt...well... different somehow. Not necessarily special either! I felt invisible.

My striving for perfection and people-pleasing always became a stress to me. I would feel everyone's pain in my heart and it was unbearable at times.

I just so badly wanted to be acknowledged for who I was...but in my mind, that was not good enough and my awkwardness and sensitivity as a young child were overwhelming with no outlet other than the sanctuary of my bedroom.

I was a slightly chubby girl as well and was often teased about it. This didn't help my already very fragile being, that struggled to understand the intensity of my inner world.

My fantasy bubble was my favorite place to be. It was my way of coping, for a long time. My bedroom and its purple walls were so covered with posters of Donny Osmond and David Cassidy, you could barely see the walls!!! I am aging myself here! I know! I had every vinyl album they had too! I loved music, even then, as I could escape and it would calm my soul.

But amongst all the posters every morning, I would open my eyes to see that infamous picture that many of us baby boomers had, one of the beautiful guardian angel with huge white wings standing behind, and watching over two children crossing a bridge. Remember that one? This was the beginning of my love of the celestial world of angels!

Some mornings, I would literally feel like that very angel in the picture was standing over my bed, looking at me!

I know it was my very own personal guardian angel and other beautiful divine spirits! Many times I would hear distant music or bells as if to wake me from my sleep, gently and with love. They knew back then that my highly sensitive nervous system needed them.

Grandma was an Empath! Who knew?

Another place I always felt safe and understood was with my Italian grandmother Rose, my maternal grandmother. She would come every Sunday for dinner and I would be so excited to greet her at the door to not only get the "ice milk" bars she brought because she said they were less fattening but to also ask her if she had any new "ghost" stories to tell tonight?! She always had this twinkle in her eye and there was an undeniable understanding I received from her like no other. She has undoubtedly been my first experience with the energy of a sensitive Empath. At that time, I didn't understand that my desire to escape in my room often was because I am an Empath too.

EMPATH: someone who is highly attuned to the emotions and feelings of those around them....including physical symptoms. An empath can also actually empathize so strongly that they will take on the energy of others within their own body without realizing it.

Grandma Rose suffered from depression often, but it was fleeting. She was labeled as a hypochondriac because she would often complain of various unknown, undiagnosed ailments that would come upon her all of a sudden and then leave almost as quickly. She was a total loner most of the time and loved it that way.

She was often sadly misunderstood and back then, not much was yet mainstream about spiritual gifts and the spiritual world. Thank goodness it's very different now! Psychics and mediums in the 60s and early 70s were almost labelled unnatural, occultism or worse!

She would often communicate to me with no words ....almost telepathically. Often I would hear her voice in my head and look up to see her winking at me! She was testing me!!

She was a devout Catholic but that didn't stop her from telling the best stories of her visitations with spirits!!! I would try to place myself in her stories and pretend I was her! Her stories never frightened me at all. I knew even as a little girl that the "supposed ghosts" were just deceased loved ones sending messages of love. I could feel the love and emotions within these stories....sometimes I could feel the pain they left behind before they died.

This was the beginning of my deep knowingness that LOVE is the answer. An intuitive sense that there is more than our eyes can see. Why didn't more people understand that? Or were they hiding it too?

Yes! I was an Empath.
Yes! I felt and heard angels.
Yes! I felt connected to all of the spirit worlds

Speak your truth....what does this mean?
Your soul has things to say.
Being authentic reveals the soul.
It strips the ego from fear and moves it into love.

Truth is transcending what crippled you to what made you rise!

I understand that part of speaking your truth can be filled with lots of ugly and broken pieces. It is through those cracks and imperfections that the light can enter.

What if everything you are going through is preparing you for what you're meant to be?

Maybe it is not about the happy ending. It is about the story.

"When we deny the story, it defines us.

When we own the story, we can write a brave new ending."

Brene Brown

Starting at age 16 and well into my twenties, I battled anorexia, which then became bulimia. These are eating disorders, which I now know were coping mechanisms and a cry for help. I initially loved the attention that I received from my peers for losing so much weight, but with time, it was a living hellish spiral of self-hate.

I married at 19 and had my daughter at 20. Nobody knew my secret until I finally realized one night, after wanting to leave this earth, that if I didn't get help, I would probably die.

At age 24, the healing journey began. It was time to surrender. I allowed grace into my life more than ever.

"I am not what happened to me,

I am what I choose to become."

Carl Jung

There will come a time when you think everything is finished.....

THAT is just the beginning......

I am confident to say that my connection to spirit, my angels and my innate empathic ability and intuition allowed me to find solace during my younger years.

My 30's, 40's and 50's were decades of TRUTH seeking.

They were years of great joys, but also great losses.

I became a grandma twice to two beautiful grandsons!

I also endured the loss of all my immediate family members; my father, mother, sister, husband and family dog of 13 years.

I have learned through these years that loving yourself first is the fastest way to connect to your inner wisdom that is your true essence. Spiritual growth comes almost as a series of revelations.

I have learned that there is a struggle in trying to be something you are not. That being free means being able to embrace your truth and love it so you can speak it to others.

Fear disconnects you from the source of creation.

Love Heals.

When I truly started loving myself completely and unapologetically, that is where I found strength, acceptance, hope, limitless abundance, and the ability to help others do the same.

Now at age 60, I wake up each day with so much gratitude for not only today, and what my future brings, but for the challenges that made me who I am today.

I love what I do!

So that infamous day in 2004 when I lost my corporate "job", I gained a calling. I embraced my purpose. I stepped fully into a place of empowerment and authenticity.

I never looked back and have been so blessed with an abundant business since that day. I let go of what weighed me down.

I truly feel I was being divinely guided.

I live my truth every single day. I have the ability to help and guide thousands of people all over the world with my work.

Yes! I talk to angels and spirit every single day! How lucky am I?

She who is Brave....is Free....

Thank you for reading my story. Keep shining your Light!

With love,
Debra

DEBRA DASARO

Debra has been guiding clients since 2004 driven by her innate ability and desire to dig deeper into the reasons why they are not living their truest, highest selves. She believes we all possess a special gift and its our destiny to share these gifts.

Debra has advanced training in Spiritual Counselling, is a Spiritual Psychology facilitator and a Certified Soul Coach. She has found her greatest gift in helping others is through her deep connection to Spirit and Angels.

Angels are the umbrella over all the work she does with her clients.

Debra gives Psychic and Mediumship readings and does healing work with clients all over the world. She is a certified Angel Intuitive and channel, Crystal and Reiki energy healer and Infinite Possibilities facilitator.

Debra lives in NJ and is a proud mother and grandmother to a beautiful daughter and two grandsons. They are her inspiration for it all.

Website: www.WhiteLightAngel.com
Facebook: www.facebook.com/debra.dasaro
Instagram: www.instagram.com/debradasaro

6

NATASHA ARATHOON

THE DOVES

I was feeling blessed and in a state of pure love and devotion several weeks after giving birth to my daughter Chloe. Warm feelings of nurture, kindness, care and love, filled my whole being. I felt such delight that I had delivered this Divine Angel into the world. In just a number of weeks, however, my world was shattered in an instant.

My mother called me one morning from her workplace asking if I could check up on Dad. Some workmen at my parent's home had phoned her to say he was acting quite peculiarly. Dad had been digging out a tree root and he incessantly kept repeating, "I've got to get it out. I've got to get it out."

I arrived at my parents' home to find my father on his bed displaying what could have been a scene from the film "The Exorcist". Dad was continually swivelling his neck from right to left. His tongue kept flopping out of his mouth and his eyes were rolling back into his head. I was shocked and scared as dad wasn't responding to me at all. As a nurse, I knew he was having a cerebral event. I also knew I had to act quickly. I called an ambulance and the paramedics came within a matter of minutes. While assisting Dad onto the gurney he had a grand mal seizure (a seizure which causes violent muscle contractions and loss of consciousness). It was one of the most distressing events I have ever had to endure.

Unfortunately, the situation didn't get any better. A trail of blood reflected a battle of wills that took place due to Dad's incoherence, as the nurses tried to administer sedation. It was an extremely sad time, yet I recall baby Chloe wrapped in her cocoon in the capsule. She was calm and peaceful, a ray of light, unaware of the dark situation that was going on around her.

At the hospital, my mother and I waited nervously before the doctor took us into his little room. "It's a Glioblastoma, a highly aggressive brain tumour that doubles it's size every two weeks," he said. The diagnosis instilled a sense of fear inside me and a knowing that it was going to be a challenging road ahead.

I recalled Dad saying on numerous occasions, "If anything ever happens to me just push me out on my surfboard. I never want to have to go to a nursing home". So we respected his wishes and nursed him at home.

Through many session's of chemotherapy, radiotherapy and a number of neurological surgeries Dad was determined to keep living the dream of being 'The Sea Dog' . My father's courage, inspiration and love of surfing was something to be in awe of during the last year of his life. Despite it all, Dad continued surfing his favourite haunts off the coastline near his home on Sydney's Northern Beaches.

I recall Dad's last wave at Collaroy Beach. Dad was paralysed down the right side of his body. It was genuinely supernatural to witness how he dragged his body and longboard down to the ocean, let alone haul his body up to ride a wave. It brought tears to my eyes and a pain in my heart when Dad came out of the ocean that day. He staggered up the sand to me and mumbled a jumble of words. His speech had rapidly deteriorated, yet my intuition knew what he was trying to say, "That was my last wave". And that it was.

The final week of Dad's life was profound for me. I knew him as a quiet, reserved type of man, a good provider for his family and someone who had an enduring love for the ocean. Yet I had not experienced such love on a personal level from my father until during his transition. The day before he died, is one that I will never forget. Looking up at me he had light emitting from his eyes directly into mine. His eyes were like laser beams of love, a type of love that I had never ever experienced from him before. At that moment, I felt all the love that my father was unable to express throughout his life, flow to me. It was sincerely angelic. I really got to see at that moment, that the eyes are truly the 'Windows of the Soul.' My courageous father passed in 2003.

After Dad's transition, I wasn't in the best space emotionally. After nursing Dad, nursing a newborn and nursing 84 elderly patients in a low care facility. I felt exhausted. I could see I had been giving love and care to everyone else except myself. I felt like I was just floating through life like a sensitive feather in the wind.

Then one particular event changed for me dramatically. I recollect walking past a Cafe and there was a woman inside that caught my eye. I knew her from the local area. She was sitting peacefully and joyfully with her toddler and newborn. I stood by the door watching, mesmerised by the captivating energy that was radiating from this heavenly woman. I knew viscerally that something was different about her. She had a glow, a bright energy and golden aura. I stood bewildered, I could sense an uplifting sense of happiness and enchantment within her. I was then guided by some unknown force that propelled me to go over. I was apprehensive, and I knew I had to talk to her. I walked over and introduced myself. "You look amazing. There is a radiance and shine about you. What have you been doing?"

"Thank you" she said. Happy to engage, Anna-Mete continued, "I just did this amazing course two months ago and it has changed my life."

I knew at that moment that I too had to do the course, and that it would change my life as well. The old saying "When the student is ready the teacher appears" was ringing loudly in my mind. I didn't know what the course was about, I did intuitively know that it was going to dramatically transform my life.

I arrived at the course with feelings of suspense, excitement and trepidation, not knowing a soul except for the sweet Danish girl Anna-mete who invited me.

There was an air of nervousness amongst all the waiting participants congregated in the foyer of the hotel. No one was making eye contact and there was a surreal aroma looming in the air. We then entered an expansive room where the course was to be held. We sat in silence until the educator entered and commenced the unfolding.

Through the three and a half-day course I was open, honest and I participated to the best of my ability. There was an expectation of deep sharing and connection which the participants embraced. The teaching was concentrated with hours of spoken theory, supplemented with whiteboard facts and flip chart knowledge. The processes we engaged in evoked a deep sense of compassion within me, more than I'd experienced in all my years of nursing.

With nearly 100 people in the room, I had a fast-track evolution into seeing myself in everyone. I found myself surrendering and releasing all the negative events, experiences, mental dialogue and programming that had accumulated in my mind and body over my lifetime. There were tears, there was laughter, and there were heart palpitations too. There was continued nurture and support behind the scenes, and I knew I had to trust the process. To go with the flow and have faith that everything would work out.

They were long days and evenings, and on the way home I got lost as there was a soup of thoughts and feelings swirling around my system. Unusual impulses of wanting to clean the house and the car were occurring. I realised this external drive was a reflection of me cleaning and clearing out my inner world.

Returning the next day, there were humbling encounters of grown men opening up with their vulnerabilities, honest accounts of their hardships, setbacks and lowest points in their lives. They demonstrated a sense of humility that was most endearing, and this paved the way in allowing me to open up with mine. The course was a wake-up call, alerting me to the fact that I had been living in my mind and had been listening to the defeatist tapes of my intellect. I saw clearly that I had been living in the past and believing illusory thoughts.

I opened up to the acceptance of everyone and everything in my life. I realised I was the creator of my life and that whatever I thought about I brought about. This truth was freeing and invigorating. It took me to a place of living a life I had always wanted. Fulfilling the dreams of what I loved and being of service in the best way possible.

On the last day of the course as I stood in front of what felt like a whole stadium of people, I felt a surge of energy building in my mind and body. I had the most mystical experience of my lifetime. I was scared to express myself and it felt like a push-pull or tug of war of energy going on inside of me. Intuitively I knew this sharing was for my highest good but it felt like a volcano was about to erupt and I couldn't hold on any longer. With gentle encouragement from the facilitator, I released some of my most challenging, moving and sensitive events of my past.

As I shared my experiences, I saw a multitude of doves flying around the ceiling. It was an incredible mystical experience. I was witnessing a plethora of pure white angelic flutter. Here I was being given an otherworldly, magical, gift. One of a supernatural, transcendental kind.

It was affirming to learn that the 'Dove' is a messenger of love and healing. It represents peace of the deepest kind, and of compassion. I felt such a joyful transition, a spiritual renewal and a sense of freedom.

We all congregated and celebrated at the hotel bar after the course. The energy in the air was electric, the joy within everyone insurmountable. A momentous night to remember.

Coming back to the 'real' world I noticed I didn't have a voice in my head. This absence of inner dialogue continued for many months. I had an immense amount of energy, I felt extremely happy and that I had a heart that had bloomed like a lotus flower to its fullest expression.

In my nursing role, I was in charge of an 84-bed aged care facility. On the first day back after the course, I walked into the nurse's clinic and no sooner had I put my bag in the cupboard when a flock of nurses gathered around me, excitedly shooting various questions at me:

"Have you been in an orgy all night?"

"What drugs are you on?"

"What has happened to you?"

That was when I had the deep realisation that we are all energy and that I was vibrating highly like a flower, and the nurses had come to taste the nectar. My energy centres had become aligned, and I was high on life. Even my mother was in amazement and had said, "You've been brainwashed by this course and the people in it." My response was "Yes, my brain has been washed. It's been cleansed of all the negative programming, experiences and events of the past". I had become someone else.

After the course, it was like I lived three years in the space of one year. I woke at 5:40 am every morning, with a smile on my face and a joy for life. I walked every morning for an hour and I would affirm "I am happy, healthy, trim and abundant and only good comes my way." I trimmed down and let go of 20kgs. I was healthy in mind, body and spirit and could only see the beauty in everything.

Raindrops became diamonds on trees when it rained. My connection with animals was profound, and I saw the magnificence and true essence of everyone. I came to realise that we are mirrors of the Universe, literally.

I truly loved my nursing job with all the oldies, so work was fulfilling.

It wasn't long however before the facility was shut down due to shaky foundations. It was old and hazardous, and all the staff were made redundant. Fear overtook everyone yet I found it exciting as it would mean a new chapter in my life.

I had many realisations after the course. The main one was that I was the creator of my life and that I can create anything. It was all about intention and feeling good. The way I see it, my thoughts go out into the Universe and my emotions magnetise back whatever is in my sub conscious. It was important to know I needed to tap into those good feeling thoughts.

My intuition was telling me I was nearing the end of my nursing career and that I was going to leap into new horizons. I just wanted to make sure that I had no doubt that it was time. I decided to use my thoughts and feelings to create the best nursing job I could imagine. I consulted my heart during meditation and then wrote down exactly what I wanted:

Registered Nurse in charge of a low care facility around 24 beds

Working three days per week

Hours 9-5 pm

Working with a kind, warm-hearted team

Situated near the beach and close to home earning around $800 per week I then surrendered, let go and felt inspired, knowing it was only a matter of time until it manifested. Then a couple of days later the miracle happened. The local newspaper, which I never read was on the dining table. I acted on the urge to flip it open. From the positions vacant page jumped out a Registered Nurse Job:

Wanted. RN in charge, 22 bed hostel, three days per week, 8-4 pm, $800 gross weekly, Northern Beaches.

That was it. Here was the job.

The next step was programming my mind that the interview was going to be the best that I had ever experienced. I meditated and visualised how I wanted it to proceed. I would connect openheartedly with the Director and exhibit that I was the one for the position.

It was an uplifting interview, and I was offered the job. What I envisaged in my mind became a reality in my outer world. To seal the deal, the people I worked with were open, caring and charismatic. The hostel was close to home, it had a lovely view of the beach and was a clean and fresh environment.

I worked for a year at the hostel, and it was enjoyable, yet there was a part of me that was hungry for more. I had a knowing that I was destined to give more of myself in service in a unique, inspiring and even more heartfelt way. I felt bound to work in a deeper, more personally fulfilling area. I started tapping into the broader meaning of life, by asking the questions: "Who am I? Why am I here? What is my purpose in life?"

This enquiry allowed me to move towards what I truly loved. A field where I could inspire, empower, love, nurture and support others to heal. I knew there was more for me to tap into, channel, learn and gain knowledge about.

I studied many modalities. I investigated various spiritual teachings and had several mentors. I delved into the mystical and the psychic senses. Meditation and connecting to the Divine became a daily practice. Massage therapy and intuitive bodywork became a love, as did Psychosomatic Therapy and Evolutionary Astrology. I had had a penchant for occult and metaphysical wisdom since I was very young and had a knowing that we are magical beings ourselves, creating our reality. Our thoughts and feelings are our magic wand, channelling focused energy to manifest our dreams and desires. I learned it was imperative to realise that we are the Light and truth within and to spread the loving service that we choose to do and keep our hearts open.

My box of tricks now consists of various methods and techniques in supporting people to be inspired and to fulfil what they love. I feel blessed by the foundation established through decades of nursing. This provided a great base for me to move into a broader healing circuit.

From one-on-one deep healing sessions, to conducting group workshops and programs to creating The women's Empowerment summit; all have played a part in the unfolding of my journey through life.

There have been many insights I've gained over the years and these are my most significant:

Trust your intuition. If it feels right, go with it. The right people cross your path at the right time.

Be grateful, open your heart, have the intention and watch the miracles appear.

Trust, surrender, release and let go, the recipe for transformation.

When you wake up, get up.

Have a daily morning routine. This supports getting beyond the self and into the heart. Eg: meditation, walking and gratitude practice.

Have buddy support, friendship, mentors and collaboration. Be around people who raise you up, and back you up.

Do what you love and have compassion.

Rehearse your future.

Don't complain, blame or gossip as it lowers vibration and sends out harmful energies.

See the benefits in the challenges of life. When you look deep enough the darkest times become your biggest blessings.

Be vulnerable. It is the birthplace between pain and joy.

And lastly, cherish your memories. My father playing with my daughter is a golden one!

NATASHA ARATHOON

Natasha is a heartfelt intuitive healer, Evolutionary Astrologer, Inspired teacher, and self discovery specialist.

She has worked in the healthcare industry for over 35 years encompassing nursing, massage, Psychosomatic Therapy and the psychic senses.

Natasha creates workshops for women on deep self-discovery and transformation and supports participants to fulfil their passion and purpose. She created The Women's Empowerment Summit to promote women in their businesses and support them in gaining clarity, direction and loving intention in their lives.

A Specialised Health Practitioner at Elysia Wellness Retreat in the Hunter Valley. Natasha runs 'Inspired Insight' sessions and is a guest speaker. She also runs Intuitive Astrological Sessions online and one-on-one healing sessions in person.

Natasha is a loving mother, daughter, sister and friend to many, who cherishes her time at the beach and in the ocean on Sydney's Northern Beaches.

Website: www.beinspiredwithnatasha.com

7

VICKI REINER

THE COMPLEXITY OF MADNESS AND THE GRACE OF LOVE AND INTUITION

My firstborn son was experiencing a mental breakdown. This was a new reality that we were not used to yet. If ever one could get used to such a thing...

I woke up to find him missing from the apartment we were staying in, while I was teaching for the weekend out of town. I assumed he would return soon. Maybe he went for a walk on the beach? I went off to teach my class that day in the area and assumed he would be back when I finished for the day. He did not return that day. I became concerned - quite concerned, and then:

My Intuition speaks. Intuition has little to no effort to it. It comes from a place that is pure spirit. Intuition does not have to consult our worries of the day, or our lists of things to do to be more perfect before it gives us an idea, answer, picture, or message that comes like a flash and feels perfectly correct.

Sometimes intuition uses pictures to communicate (clairvoyance). Sometimes it uses other realms to communicate through. Clearly, I saw a credit card in my mind. I pondered this - My credit card!

Hmmm... Yes! I remembered that he had my credit card with him! I was so happy to remember this detail. I was then able to track him by any purchase he had made with my card, so I had an idea where he was in this new city! And more than that, I knew he was ALIVE then! What a relief! Thank-you Intuition. I knew he was struggling with reality. I did not know how bad it was yet.

My youngest son and I went looking for him as night fell. This was the second night he was lost in an unknown city. We decided we had to take action. It seemed overwhelming to tackle this as night was falling. Where would we begin? I barely knew the area where I was teaching.

Since I had been tracking his whereabouts with the credit card, I knew the area he was in. We drove around a park near where a church he had been to recently, was located. He had expressed a resonant fondness for the wonderful charismatic Reverend of this church. I had a feeling about this. My Intuition was speaking to me... We got out of the car to check around the park.

This park was very, very dark. It felt ominous. There was no lighting at all. We lingered there not knowing what to do, but just standing, listening for hints from nature or the wind, or the moon, or the leaves, or within - anywhere. We had felt hopeful when we began and full of the bravado of love; "We WILL find him!" We will just use our instincts and intuition. That's the only hope we had and from the moment starting out we felt aligned, Mother and Son on a mission of love.

We stood there in the darkness, and neither one of us felt the impulse to move from the spot we were on. We just stood in silence looking into the pitch-black dark park in all directions - frozen at the task we had undertaken in the nightfall. We lost hope for the moment and we left, finally. The shock had set in for us both, and the fear of losing our loved one was there in silence. I refused to believe it, but it was there. I was physically and psychically exhausted. It felt good to surrender to the night. I just knew my intuition would return tomorrow.

Intuition guides us to seek our wholeness. It searches for our instinctual and gut-level connections to the natural world, our cycles of life, death, transformation, and our place in the cosmos. Our Intuition is very efficient, it goes directly to knowing!

"Your Son is in the Hospital", the Policeman said through the phone. We found your son in the park screaming in the bushes, (the very park where we had stood in the dark) he reported. "We took him to the hospital as we knew he needed help. Your number was in his pocket." I cried deep tears of relief. Humanity and care from the Big City Police. My lost son deserved this kind of help, and the Police in that area had been clearly trained to recognize mental health and treat him with care instead of indignity as so many other areas treat the mentally ill. My heart lifted for the first time in three days. My eyes closed as I thanked in silence any forces that were helping us all reunite. We found out later that he was hiding in a bush just yards away from where his brother and I stood frozen that night when we went looking for him! Intuition led us there. In all of this big city, we had found the very place he was that night but did not know it cogently. We never thought to call out his name!

Intuition does not consult our fears. It leaves them be. It does not consult with our limits. It moves them aside. It does not honor our parents, spouses, or children above ourselves. It speaks to us directly when it arrives. It knows when to arrive.

My son lay in the hospital gurney in a hollow, sensory deprived, concrete-walled empty holding space. Our eyes met. He smiled with the relieved, lost, moist eyes of a much younger, sweet boy, earnest and very, lost and confused. Maybe he was in this reality, this dimension? Maybe... He gazed at me with that lost, distant, but yet present love and said with an exhausted small voice "Mom, you are here. They told me you were dead."

The "voices" he was hearing are relentlessly cruel and dark. They had repeatedly told him I was dead. My heart broke into tender tears for my lost sweet son. Lost in more ways than one. He then fell silent and passed out in utter exhaustion. He can sleep now, he is safe, I whispered to myself. For the moment anyway.

There is dignity in complexity. I witnessed this in all of this crazy world our family had entered since my son had entered the land of the lost and confused. My constant question to myself, though silent, was, "How am I going to get through this?" How do I keep him safe while I learn and research and navigate a mental health system that is so broken and incomplete in helping those it serves. How do I take care of me and my other Son, and make money somehow in the sane moments, and keep myself sane and calm? The mental health system, so far, is a travesty. A travesty of proportions unfathomable to me. They have a very short list of tools and then we are on our own to navigate madness, fear, safety, and pure insanity day by day, night by night. The truth became apparent. No one understands this illness. It is still a mystery. They do their best. There are just no real answers.

Intuition is the best and maybe only tool I had in my toolbox for this time in my life. We have to give intuition space to arrive though. After I struggled with my analyzer till my brain hurt to figure out what was happening, I let go of the effort to understand. I just let go! And magically, as if I just gave in to the wonder of life, then Intuition arrived with its signature voice of "Aha!". The light turned back on inside, I took a deep needed breath. Intuition could transcend the hopelessness, and the craziness. When my mind could not understand a world gone mad, my intuition could offer the solution. "He is safe, you are safe, just breathe." And simple as that, I took a much-needed deep breath and smiled with renewed courage and hope.

The ambulance arrived. The staff lifted my son onto the gurney and transferred him to the ambulance. It's busy and fast and no one at all is interested in talking with me. I seem invisible. They are not interested in my questions. "Where are you taking him? Where is he going? Don't you have to talk with me?" No one even responds. They don't look at me at all. Are they trained to not respond at all I wonder? This appears to be normal to them. Am I invisible?

My Intuition speaks: "Just stay calm, grounded, stay alert...more will come."

The ambulance takes off and I am told by one of the nurses that I have no rights at all until my son can sign a release form to let me know where he is going. A moment of sheer panic and a realization of the madness I am listening to just silences my voice. Even my inner voice cannot find sounds to utter. I stand in a moment of emptiness. A stunned silence trying to understand a reality that just put my son into an ambulance in front of me and pretended that his Mother, had no right at all to know what was happening or where they were taking him. The doors of the ambulance shut and I was left speechless and feeling lost and in shock. I began to wonder how I navigate this insane scene and world of hospital craziness that rivaled the madness my son was in. I'm standing right there. It took me three days to find him, and no one acknowledges me at all. No one! And they cannot answer my questions. "Where are you taking him? How can I find him? Why are you completely ignoring me?" Not a word, they just do their job, strapping him onto a gurney and loading him into an ambulance. I don't even say goodbye or let him know that I will be with him where he is going. I don't KNOW where he is going!!! Pure crazy madness again. The ambulance leaves and the loud sirens begin to disappear.

I realize that I am standing there alone looking at the empty night where the ambulance had just been. I have a moment of fear and sadness. Where did they take him? All the staff helpers have walked away and gone back to their jobs. No one says a word to me or even acknowledges the comfort I may need. I'm simply there, alone, in a kind of slow shock, and feeling cold, very cold.

A nurse takes me aside as I wander in from the door opening where the ambulance had been, wondering what I do now. She quietly puts a ripped-off note in my hand and walks by. She can't say too much, it is clear. It is against protocol apparently to let me even know where he is going. WHAT? This is my son!! She had heart and gave me the name of the facility where they were taking him. She first had given me a lecture in anger asking "why was he not on meds?". She was angry and scolding and self-righteous. It was clear to me that she did not know and was not interested in asking what had happened. That angry, self-righteous attitude never really helps anyone understand, but it gave her power over the real truth that no one really knows what to do with the reality of madness. Her fear and inability to put it into any known box for her own internal support were clear to me. It hurts, but it's not personal.

Intuition speaks: It has a new life to give me, a more open outlook, an expanded perspective I never considered. My inner voice is a gift of the moment. A moment when we move beyond logic that is just not big enough to hold the soul. Intuition whispers to me, "It does induce fear in all of us." "Yes", I thought, "it does". It calms me to acknowledge the truth. Truth gives space. It does not need answers.

What does it mean to lose your mind? Is part of it there? Is he just on a journey, a trip of sorts inside a reality where each frame may be recognizable, but the whole scene makes no sense? It has no anchor in our reality to make sense. It is outside of understanding through our senses and sensibilities. It's an empty frame on the wall that we stare at and try our best to understand and put in context or give it a reality that we can hold. There are moments of brilliance in this madness that give us the hope we all need.

Intuition speaks; Hope - This is in the realm of Intuition. Intuition does not have to be logical. It does not rest in the same vibration as logic. Intuition bypasses logic. Logic cannot hold intuition. However, intuition can easily hold logic. It then transcends it and opens it into a grand sunset of epic proportions that make sense on a whole different level than logic can ever grant favor to.

Hope is the only reality I can hold onto, ungrounded, distant, shaky at best, but the best and only strength I can find. I am grateful to believe in hope and use it as my anchor to find strength in this crazy maze and struggle for my son's life and sanity in an equally crazy medical world that has to uphold patient rights above their own emotional understanding that this is not "right". They have to ignore my existence completely and close their own hearts to comply with patient laws. He is not aware enough to sign a form so that I can know his whereabouts or even ask a question on his behalf. I have no rights to his life. Shocking! Just shocking! I almost crumbled to the floor as the ambulance shut the door in front of me and the men jump inside and drive away. I stand there wondering if this is a nightmare I am in. Will I awaken soon? Could I even dream up a nightmare this fragmented and cruel without making any sense?

Intuition arrives again: The horror of this moment is almost too much. I ground myself again and move into hope and my undying belief that I will find a way through this. My inner voice is speaking, "Expand your Awareness". It is not wishful thinking. It is my inner voice helping me through this. I can relax a bit inside almost immediately to allow for expansion.

Safety was becoming a relative idea in my new life living with madness. He was safe for the moment, somewhere, in a hospital somewhere, in a bed, pumped full of drugs to help him sleep and find calm... maybe.

The rights are written for the patient. Even when the patient can't speak for themselves. My son went mute for two days, comatose, unable to speak or understand. I called the hospital that I was given the name of, to ask how he was. The attendant said they cannot tell me if he is even a patient in their hospital. "If he is here, he will have to sign forms that say we can talk with you on his behalf."

How long do I wait? What if he cannot remember his own reality when he wakes up? Where are my rights? I was told that if he does not sign or is unable to, he would be signed out probably within three days. That's the usual amount of time to get him drugged enough to let him go. LET HIM GO?? Do you mean if he cannot sign or remember who he is, that you can just open the front door and let him walk outside with nothing and no one to care for him? No money, phone, nothing? How would I find him? It was too much to take in. Yet, this was the honest, crazy reality. I tried to sleep, and comprehend a system so crazy that it equaled my son's insanity. I was beginning to comprehend how the lost souls are just walking around the streets wandering and talking to themselves, not knowing where they are or how they got there.

Sometimes when life is just too big and far too crazy to comprehend, it feels like the world stops spinning and a hazy roulette wheel is spinning with an indignant, otherworldly mist and way off-kilter at that.

Intuition came to me: I turn to Spirit for guidance. I trust, I ground, I move within, into a pure stillness that I have come to know intimately. A space to ask the BIG questions that have no earthly answers. What do I do next? I am so thankful for the years I have spent in meditation and finding peaceful stillness to ask the really big questions of life. How would I have navigated this realm without it? "Expand your awareness" I hear once again... I know this as solid wisdom.

That night, I thank my inner strength and am glad that this is a very developed part of my being. I am known for my calm strength. I wonder, was this a gift from my higher self at birth? Did some part of me or some guide somewhere actually know what I would have to navigate in the upcoming life I had planned? The seemingly empty thoughts and inner questions like this seem silly but are so useful - even if never answered fully. They have to be asked.

Intuition speaks with the certainty I need: Be brave, stay strong. Call him by name in your inner voice. Say hello to his soul that you know so well. "Yes!" I hear myself say. My knowingness gains strength and I am sure I can manage this strange world I find myself in. I whisper his name inside, calling him from within. It feels good. I feel like I connect to him.

He awakened on the third day and signed the papers for me to talk with the staff. OMG! Yes!

My inner voice speaks again with its simplicity of wisdom: "Recovery is not efficient: It won't happen on my wanted timeline. Just love him, just love him..." Yes", I can do that easily I whisper to myself. Love is big enough to handle this.

My family has healed in ways immeasurable as a result of the trauma we have been through for 10yrs. together. Any small improvement in someone's life changes their world, and the worlds of those around them. With this perspective, I feel blessed.

VICKI REINER

Vicki Reiner is a masterful teacher of Intuition and Clairvoyance. She teaches programs to see your truth, find your answers, and navigate life with your inner awareness alive and available at every moment. Walking through life with your eyes open is a must, walking with your third eye open is a life altering event! She has been teaching programs for the past 25yrs, as well as giving individual readings, hands on healings, and aura healings. She teaches classes from beginning up to mastery of being able to "read" others as well. Her soft and clear understanding of this work is unique. Vicki believes we all have this "gift". *"It is not a gift of the few, it is a gift of the BODY, everybody!"* If you want to develop it, or just check it out, it is easier than you think! You can find Vicki at the links below

You can find Vicki Reiner at:
www.vickireiner.com Eye of Intuition
Vicki Reiner @Facebook.com
reinerdog@sbcglobal.net

8

ANGELA BIXBY

THIRD EYE BLIND: HOW DOES YOUR EGO BLIND YOUR INTUITION?

*T*he dream portends that she is, and has, disrespected me. It shows me that she isn't to be trusted. But I met her in a spiritual meditation group...how can she be harmful for me? And how might I distance myself from this friendship that feels too enmeshed in my life?

Intuition is a funny thing. We tend to believe it on our terms. The terms of our egos, that is. As humans we all have and always will have an ego that supports us and forms our personality. It can wreak havoc though, upon our intuition.

When our ego gets involved with our intuition, particularly in cases of self-guidance, it looks something like this, "No. That can't be true. She smiles so brightly and is always ready to help me. But she supports me when I ask her to, without judgment of me. How can my instincts to distance myself from this friend be true?"

A second way that our egos enter situations such as this and try to talk us out of listening to our intuition, is via fear. Fear is a powerful emotion that we know of as a source to keep us out of danger.

Problems arise when we allow them to rule situations that aren't with inherent danger. In the situation with this friendship—my fear sounded like this, "If I leave the friendship for no reason, will I lose other friends? What will people think when I'm no longer friends with this apparently, shiny-happy person?" And, "why would you push friends away?" Fear was trying to talk me out of my intuition, by ushering in doubt and judgment. Perhaps you can begin to see how our ego jumps in to cloud our intuition, when my intuition in this sense, was pointing me towards the exit door of this friendship.

Why is it easier to believe the intuitive nudges that say— "turn here", "don't enter that place it's not for you"—than the ones that say—"this person whom you've trusted as a friend for a decade is not really your friend?" When we have a deeper investment in a decision, a deeper emotional investment, we— frankly—have more at stake. And that means our ego has more at stake too.

This is where we, as humans, try to logically analyze what we see, versus what the unseen realms are communicating to us for our highest good. Our intuition, our psychic senses, our nudges from all of the unseen realms, is deeply valuable for us as humans. I find that when our intuition is nudging us towards change—this is the hardest, personal guidance to follow. However, it also ends up being the most rewarding.

As a professional psychic, it's quite easy for me to read for people. I'm able to paint the pictures verbally for someone, as I watch the holograms dance and sparkle in the air before me and as I listen to my guides speak to me through words, thoughts and feelings. Channeling, quite literally, higher guidance on their behalf and investigating possibilities for and with them, so that they may decide next steps in their situation(s). Clients are hiring me for this purpose and so the energy exchange is clear.

As conscious humans striving for awareness in our relationships, for example, we don't always see our own egos when they come in and cloud our intuition. It is challenging to be both consultant and client for ourselves.

Before a particular experience with a former friendship, that I'll fill you in on a bit more in subsequent paragraphs—I only ever used my intuition for others. It wasn't so much that I defied my intuition, knowingly—it is that I hadn't had a lot of hard proof of where my intuition had served me. As a result I didn't consider it as a skill to support myself very readily. This situation helped me to realize and honor the deep value of my intuition and its place in my life.

The back story is that I knew she was troubled when I met her. We had a serendipitous meeting at a spiritual meditation group in the early 2000's. After we'd met, I noticed her crying to the group leader. The 'ignorant empath' in me at the time, didn't realize that I was allowing myself to be sucked into someone else's pain so that I might lessen it for both them and me. As empaths, when we lessen pain for others, we lessen pain for ourselves. Since we feel so much of what others are experiencing, it is part of how empaths show their ignorance to their own needs while putting others' first. Funny what hindsight, wisdom and growing one's intuition can do for an 'ignorant empath'!

The friendship was fun and a delightful set of escapades, most of the time. It was a source of laughs and support and creative expression. That tearful night of connection started to explain itself as the friendship progressed through the years. I began to experience the pain under the surface that the happy facade was obscuring in her. The wholesome exterior turned to my having experiences of witnessing her risky behaviors and being let in on the inner workings of her life that belied the surface appeal. As I grew increasingly less comfortable, vocalized it on many occasions and worked to put distance there—things seemed to get stickier between us.

Fast forward to the fall of '13. I began to experience constant tinnitus in one of my ears. It carried on for many weeks, annoyingly so. As an energy healer and professional psychic, I used all of my tools including readings and healings with colleagues, dialoguing with my guides, meditation and automatic writing. None of these methods brought forth helpful guidance—until I decided to harness the power of my intuition through the dreamspace.

Dreams and the dreamspace can be lush and fertile ground for psychic connection. As we sleep, so too do our egos! Sleeping egos mean that the guards are off duty. The walls are down and the unseen realms find all sorts of connection with us while we sleep. We often have visitations from dead loved ones, answers to our day-to-day bumps in life, journeys with our astral and other spiritual bodies, to realms that allow us to assist in all sorts of purposes. Dreamspace is where I turn to problem-solve when all other methods aren't as fruitful.

One of my favorite practices to employ when facing the challenge of personal decisions where my emotions are involved, is that of putting my dreams to work for me. As a professional psychic, I assume an emotional bias in queries about myself. I own and acknowledge that I might influence my intuition—which would mean not really honoring or listening to what my intuition is trying to tell me. I've had great success with getting answers within the dreamspace for personal conundrums. This tinnitus challenge seemed to be a great opportunity for me to open up to this practice.

The ear ringing challenge at minimum, had me knowing that I wasn't hearing something, some message, some warning, some wisdom that was meant for me. So prior to sleep one night I wrote in my journal — "Dear angels and guidance team, what is it that I am not hearing? What is the message that this tinnitus is trying so hard to tell me?" I added, "I am intending and asking that you bring me the answers in my dreamspace tonight. I am open to how you'd like to bring this information to me, whether literally or metaphorically." I then went to sleep and awaited guidance and messaging from the unseen realms.

What ensued in the dreamspace was rather amazing. Now, knowledge of how I dream and how I receive messages is important here. I don't dream literally. My dreams since childhood have been largely, metaphorical and allegorical. Many people dream literally and prophetically, at least when they do they know that it is more literal than metaphor and likely prophetic. While I've had extremely occasional prophetic dreams—in this case I had a specific focal point with my query of, 'what am I not hearing?' My knowing of how my dreams tend to communicate with me was key here—note this for your own use of the dreamspace for your queries.

The dream that ensued was one of falling in love, betrayal and heartbreak. The betrayal in the dream, was by said 'friend' in real life. She showed up literally in this dream, surprisingly, as I dream so metaphorically, and with a smile. She even took the time in the dream, to justify the betrayal on her part to explain the heartbreak on my part. She did so with a smile and an air of arrogance, as though she had known what was best for me and had acted accordingly. She also acted as though her behavior was above reproach. As I woke, I was reminded of a time when something along these lines had happened in real life with her. While rising I declared aloud to my guidance team, "Ah! It's in my highest good to break up with this friend. This is what you've been trying to tell me with the tinnitus for the past six weeks."

The tinnitus stopped immediately and didn't come back. I had clearly received the answer that my guidance team had shown me in my dreamspace. More importantly, I 'got it', acknowledged it and a few moments later agreed to tend to this 'break up'. I knew that following through would be important if I didn't want the tinnitus to return. I was given a deep sense of comfort and knowing from my guidance team that there wasn't anything for me to do yet. That the opportunity for a friend-separation would occur naturally and soon.

Within about three weeks' time, the opportunity arose. This personality was clearly feeling my distance and was working hard to lure me back into a more enmeshed space. Through a series of events and communications, not always high-vibed and neatly packaged—we managed to separate as friends.

While this flavor of drama may be unappealing to most of us—it is so common for 'ignorant empaths' in recovery. How we communicate, what we sense from the other person's emotional responses to said communication—all of this comes into play. Particularly when we are working hard to rise above old patterns and listen to our intuition.

The steps to take in working with one's intuition for a symptom such as the one that I was experiencing—(nagging tinnitus for weeks on end)—are as follows.

Identify the 'symptom' or 'message'. In my case it was tinnitus. In yours it may be a repeating message to move on, a headache, a level of situational anxiety, or something as random as a repeating number or a color that is presenting repeatedly as a message for you. Once identified, decide how you'd like to pose a question to your guidance team/angels/the unseen realms, as a method for welcoming in their assistance in your dreamtime. Keep the question clear and succinct. Stay humble and be prepared to engage with your guidance team upon waking. To engage—acknowledge the solution presented. Decide too—what sort of actions steps that you will take as a result of the solution presented in your dream. Then commit to acting in the coming days or weeks, depending upon your situation.

This commitment to taking action and then taking action comes in many forms. It may be committing to journaling out your feelings about the solution. The solution may be presented as therapy or talking to a trusted confidante—so that the action would be bringing the issue to a therapist or confidante. The action step may be something as specific as to—throw away the piece of jewelry that so-and-so gifted to you, or as broad as to—spend more time in nature. Decide from your presented solution, what action step that you will take.

This serves two purposes. The first being moving forward and closing the loop on this process of asking for help from the dreamspace. The second is a demonstration of respect and gratitude for the guidance team that brought this solution forward for you. Cultivating relationships with the unseen realms and your guidance team are similar to human relationships. You'll get out of them, what you put into them.

Living more deeply in tune with my intuition took off from this experience. In a gradual fashion I chose to trust more in the guidance that I was receiving for myself in my own life. One of the best gifts of this experience is that my clairaudience came on-line more strongly because of my freshly found trust in my process. I began to hear spirit in my head as though we were having continuous conversation! As I would consult these guides in my head, first on mundane things like grocery lists or routes to travel on my commute, it too grew stronger for me.

I'm fascinated still, by what we will readily trust and what we'll scrutinize. It turns out I spent a lot of time scrutinizing my knowing. I saw this as I engaged more fully with the clairaudience. It was entertaining to learn what I would heed and what I would dismiss. I experienced this guidance in such a loving and fascinating way. It felt like guidance was showering down upon me like a waterfall. Sure there were a few stones and such that clanked down into my fields with the knowing, these offered texture to the experiences. Over time these bits of debris that came in with the clarity ended up adding to how grounded my intuition felt for me. The splashes of wisdom when followed—brought more knowing and confidence in. The trust in guidance like—change your plans tonight you are meant to catch a call that is coming to you—became exciting as though I were receiving clues in a scavenger hunt that were about me and my life. The process has strengthened and snowballed over the past years.

Living fully aligned with my intuition makes my past seem quite foreign. I waste no time on—why not? Are you sure? Instead, hopping right to the guidance that flows through naturally now. The messages are less like being sprayed by a waterfall and occasionally thumped on the head with a stone—and now feel much more like swimming in an ocean of knowing and allowing it to support me and guide me with its own waves and tides. It takes the guesswork out of situations yet still leaves room for the mystery and excitement of life.

The reactions that I get are funny at times. I was already a confident person and now my loved ones do look at me sideways. Wondering if I'm being cavalier or merely listening to said guidance. They certainly remain respectful and watch quietly in amazement to see how the messages work magic in my life. I love the enthusiasm that catches like a brush fire in those close to me, as they too discover the value in following their intuition. As we act from a place of deeper knowing, without the analysis and doubt that our ego tries to throw at the intuitive messages that we are receiving, we feel more naturally satisfied.

One of the most rewarding outcomes of following the guidance that my intuition offers up—is that I get to affirm for others their own processes. I am a living example to all of whom I attract and work with, on how to not only train your intuition up but also these value pieces of working with it. Listening more deeply. Heeding the knowings. Trusting the process. As a poster child for—grow your intuition, grab hold of it and don't let go—I naturally teach these processes with embodied authenticity. I get to teach people to navigate their own swells while enjoying the swim. I get to demonstrate how to quiet the voice of the ego and listen to the quieter yet more solid voice of our intuition.

My hope is that the example that I've shared with you here—six or so weeks of physical discomfort, ceasing immediately upon gleaning a message from my intuition through the tool of harnessing answers from the dreamspace—will offer you hope and teaching as to how you too can work with your intuition.

There is no better tool for twenty-first century living. Our consciousness is rising as a planet and as a species. Our intuition is our best source of knowing how to proceed in life. While we grow increasingly more skeptical of external authority, we naturally need a deeper trust in our intuition. May you live life in love and from your knowing.

Website: www.energyintuit.com

ANGELA BIXBY

Living beyond the five senses has always been a part of how Angela Bixby sees and approaches the world. She is a Certified Psychic Medium with the American Federation of Certified Psychics and Mediums, which has furthered her innate skills. While Angela channels answers to client questions during each session, -- her passion is teaching people to connect to their own intuition. Through her Conscious Psychic Program , she mentors you through your own spiritual awakening process. Angela's teaching style draws upon her own experiences, as well as those of the thousands of clients and& students with whom she has had the honor of working with and teaching.

Angela holds a BA in Psychology from the University of Minnesota, a Masters Certificate in Holistic Psychology and formerly worked in healthcare. Angela enjoys creating and is the mother of two spirited, young men in Chester County, PA.

Website: www.energyintuit.com

9

JACQUI MCGINN

HOW TELLING THE TRUTH BROUGHT LIGHT
TO DARKNESS

"*I*f I see a compass today, I'll quit my teaching contract and go for it in business" I said to myself one sticky July morning in China.

I was working as an English teacher in one of the top schools in Fujian Province. A job I'd craved for over 2 years. Unhappy in my part-time Japanese teacher job in the UK, I always felt there was more I should be doing. I was fed up with constantly feeling judged and never good enough in education. The chance to teach in China had seemed like the ideal adventure to shake off this low self-esteem. But the moment I sat on the bed in my new apartment in China, I knew this wasn't the place for me.

The trip to China was through a college I worked at. I was supposed to go 9 months earlier in September 2013, but at the end of August, my boss sat me down and gave me the news that I couldn't go. For the next 9 months, it was a jerky on-again-off-again ride to finally get there. Problems mounted, delaying the trip and taking my patience to its absolute limit. Frustration burned into surrender and I let go of needing to go. After surrendering, the trip was finally on.

During this wait for China, I got the chance to go to lots more spiritual talks. One that stood out and felt serendipitous was by Robert Holden on his book "Loveability". The first activity at the event was to stand up and tell 10 different people one lovely thing that had happened in the past week.

We all stood up to start, but I had no one to talk to. Robert noticed and became my partner. The first thing that came to mind was a conversation with one of my Japanese students. We were talking about Philip Pullman's "Northern Lights" and I asked her what she thought my daemon (my soul animal companion) would be. She said a deer because I was graceful. "Graceful" was so far from how I saw myself that it really touched my heart. Robert agreed that it was lovely and shared how his beloved kids had drawn him pictures to welcome him home from a business trip.

With each recalling of something lovely, my whole body and mind softened as my heart opened, bringing a sense of peace and presence. In that altered state, I drove back home feeling uplifted and inspired, and the name "Pieces to Peace" dropped into my mind. It felt so right - the perfect name to sum up how I'd once felt shattered to pieces by trauma, and how all the learning about spirituality and healing since then had given me moments of compassion and connectedness. Little glimpses of a bigger peace that was possible.

Truth be told, my heart was still broken over leaving Japan - the place I'd called my home for over 9 years. The place I'd worked as an English teacher literally from the day after I graduated from uni. Yokohama City had been my home through one of the toughest, most life-changing, and heartbreaking years. A year whose aftershocks reverberated year on year and taught me ever more about the depths and genius of the psyche.

Moving back to the UK from Japan had been tough. Japan had changed me. I was no longer British and yet not Japanese either. I'd learned to speak Japanese fluently. I could pass for Japanese on the phone but being seen as Japanese came to feel stifling - as if an important part of me went unseen. The same was true of coming back to the UK. Being seen as British was equally stifling. I lived in a lonely no-mans-land of not being fully one thing or the other.

I found some solace in becoming a Japanese teacher at two local colleges. Being seen as the cool, unique teacher who could read all these strange symbols, soothed my outsider wounds for a while.

Being in China just made me feel even more of a lonely, lost outsider. Not speaking the language, being stared at and feeling bad about having a higher salary than my Chinese colleagues all made for an uncomfortable time. Admittedly, I did have some amazing moments there - coffee on a beautiful, vast coffee farm while chatting about Chinese philosophy, delicious homecooked meals in teachers' homes, and of course, connecting with students who named me "Meishi" (Beautiful Madder Flower).

It was never meant to be a long stay. To make sure of that, I was left feeling vulnerable when a strange man followed me. Walking along a busy shopping street, I suddenly realised I was being followed and stared back to show him I'd noticed, hoping that would be enough to shame him into stopping. It wasn't.

"He's a small man, I'm fit because I've been working out," I told myself. "I could defend myself." But then I remembered, "Shit, I don't have a mobile phone to call anyone." Vulnerability deepened at that thought of not having a way to contact anyone I knew.

I tried twice to lose him in a shop. The first time failed, the second time I managed it. After an hour or so of browsing, I came out of the shop. To my relief, I couldn't see him. But I wasn't taking any chances. I took the long way to my flat through the main school gate and past the guards at the school gate. The grand pathway to the statue of a saluting Chairman Mao had never felt so comforting. I was safe. And my decision was made - I'm not coming back to this unsafe place in September.

But there was still another decision to make. Was it time to quit my teaching contract and go for it in business and whatever "Pieces to Peace" was? That had always been the plan. I'd always thought I'd make loads of money from my Japanese skills which would help me fund a business using my healing skills.

I have no idea why I was sure I could base such a major decision on whether I'd see a compass or not, but I woke up with a strong resolve that that's how I would decide. Some inner knowing was getting ready to reveal itself.

Zhangzhou was grey, hazy and polluted. In stark contrast to the ugly grey buildings, the most beautifully painted temples were dotted around the city. Bright, vibrant colours with dragons and phoenixes, contrasted against the dirty grey, pointing the way to heavenly realms. I stopped by one of the ornate temples by the river. Looking down, I realised I was sitting on an octagon shape. The octagon being like the Feng Shui compass. Was this the compass? No, it was too much of a stretch to see it as a compass.

I carried on walking through the city, baking in hot, hazy sunshine. I came to a huge supermarket and decided to look inside for some souvenirs for friends and family. Meandering through the aisles, suddenly there it was - the compass of destiny. Just to ram home the point, it was in the wrong place. Instead of being with the other compasses, it was with the mechanical pencils - just so I'd really notice it. I didn't know it at the time, but there was more meaning in its location than I'd anticipated. Meaning that would only be revealed a few years later.

I'd got my sign. It was time to quit my teaching contract and make the leap into business.

Peace - that was my focus. It felt huge and "Pieces to Peace" as a project felt huge. I would soon find out that this was going to be one hell of a learning curve. I ran an online meditation course with two students, making the rookie mistake of cramming too much information into a short space of time. I then created Christmas meditations for peace and joy. Figuring that this was what everyone wants and they'd be so inspired by the Pieces to Peace Project that they'd come in their hundreds, or even thousands to buy the meditations and follow my social media channels.

I sold one meditation pack. I didn't even really sell that because it was a test that my mum did for me. My hopes and dreams were beginning to come crashing down. I wasn't getting an influx of healing clients either.

Disappointed and worried about money, I rejoined the childcare and education agency I'd worked at when I first got back to the UK. I loved working with little kids and students with special education needs, but the job was tinged with shame about how my business wasn't working and how I'd had to get a part-time job to make ends meet.

The keys I needed for success lay inside, within the parts of myself that I avoided and buried out of sight. But when you bury important parts of yourself, they don't disappear. They can also negatively impact the decisions you make. One of my symptoms was a disconnect from reality - the dissociation that comes with trauma - leaving your body as a way of coping with intense emotional pain. This manifested as being sucked into large, expensive programmes with slick marketing. They captured my imagination about how they would solve my financial woes and result in clearly visible signs of success - the money, the car, the house.

Again and again, I was left frustrated, feeling mislead by these courses and watching my debts deepening. Instead of listening to my body's intuitive nudges, I placed more trust in the tricksy marketing tactics that poked at my deeply buried pain and the desperate need to appear successful. I yearned to stop feeling ashamed of how unsuccessful, misunderstood and alone I felt deep inside.

During this time, the healing tools I'd learned became self-critical weapons to beat myself with. Forever the self-improvement project, I kept thinking to myself that if only I could find THE key limiting belief keeping my shameful problems in place, everything would change. I couldn't understand why I was treated so badly by life, why my dreams and visions weren't coming true. Why was I attracting ever more debt? What was wrong with me? The more I tried healing myself with belief-clearing tools like ThetaHealing and EFT, the louder other people's shaming and criticism felt.

Harsh words cut like a knife, making me feel attacked and often needing days or even weeks to recover. It was all psychic attacks, I reasoned. I was a sensitive empath whose light brought out others' shadows, I reasoned with myself. Blind to how I'd turned sacred healing tools into weapons of self-criticism for not being good enough to create a successful business or home of my own.

In a desperate attempt to get things moving towards my dreams, I tried writing a book, to disastrous effect. Convinced that it was a narcissist that pushed me over the edge in my breakdown, I chose narcissism as my topic. My writing swung from being rigidly academic to falling apart emotionally. Eventually, I handed in a shambolic mess to my book coach, who did the best she could with what was probably the worst manuscript she'd ever read. Everyone writes a shitty first draft. This was a shitty first draft on steroids.

18-months later, more warnings came that things were really not OK. Before going on holiday, I'd got my marketing system set up - at least, I thought I had. I had blogs on narcissism. I had a quiz to find out where you needed healing and a course on understanding and healing shame. It was all going to tick over and bring me new customers, while I relaxed by the sea in the sun and wrote my book.

It all fell apart disastrously. Suffering from jetlag, I discovered my website was hacked with an ominous message left in code, saying that the message had to stay or there would be consequences. Every 20 minutes I got a fake Russian email signing up to my mailing list. On top of that, my list was flagged for spam abuse because the real people were signing up and unsubscribing straight away. My mind took it all way out of proportion. It had echoes of the inner hell I'd experienced before. I felt victimised and under attack on all fronts but determined to show an outwardly peaceful face to the world.

Shaken by these events, I doubled down on trying to prove myself. I joined another expensive business course and attempted to push through the problems and the intense criticism I'd been feeling. I loved the course but it was wrong for me. Thinking I had to spend more to make it work, I signed up for an even more expensive year-long programme in another attempt to force it. Impatient to get out of debt and be seen as successful.

The programme wasn't any help. In fact, it made things worse. I thought I was joining a group where we'd be spiritually guided and following intuition, but it was rigid, head-centred business strategy that stifled intuition and creativity.

Realising the massive mistake I'd made in joining, I briefly sank into despair. Drowning in growing debt, all I could see ahead of me was gloom, despair and deepening debt. I'd sunk lower than ever.

While all seemed to be lost, life had made sure it was equipping me with more tools and surrounding me with powerful people. A few months earlier, I'd started a hypnotherapy course with an extraordinary teacher. An expert on trauma from her own childhood experiences and decades of healing. This was the teacher I needed to begin the real healing work.

Earlier on the course, she'd noticed that I had a whining, teenage-like tone to my voice when I asked a question for clarification. We worked on it during a practice session and a real piece of me returned - helping me express my deep curiosity and desire to fully grasp the essence of what she was teaching. The whinging teenager had gone and the relentlessly curious, truer version of me was unleashed - all the while helping my teacher get clearer on her own understanding through my questions.

This newer capacity to express truer thoughts helped me to harness rage I was feeling about the expensive programme I was in and how it had not lived up to the promises made on social media. I let the rage flow as I furiously typed a draft of an email. I then brought in logic to find practical examples to demonstrate the truth of what I was feeling. I wrote a powerful email that terminated the year-long contract, opening the door for others to leave too.

My core reason for leaving had been to join a 6-month writing course instead. More committed than ever to writing, I believed I'd have a book at the end of it. Except that all of my writing just seemed to be rant after rant. When on earth was this going to turn into something someone else could read?

But this was my opportunity to feel deeply into the truth of my life and what had happened. Writing helped me reflect and welcome all of my emotions. Rage, hatred, shame, envy - all given space to flow and to bring their vital messages to me. Rage ignited at injustice and unequal power dynamics. Hatred revealed deeply buried pieces of my own shadow that I'd projected onto others. Shame began to restore its role in my psyche as integrity-keeper rather than a self-berater.

Each welcomed emotion signaled to my psyche that I was ready to face the demons of my past. I was ready to begin entering the final integration and synthesis stage of an initiation that had started 16 years earlier.

The writing programme ended still with no sight of an actual book. But a familiar feeling returned. A feeling of not wanting to go on, that life had been drained of all meaning. This time, I could work with it consciously. I knew that if I tried to write reasons to stay alive that I'd just annoy myself, so I surrendered to it, writing all the reasons NOT to be alive until something shifted and the meaninglessness began to lift, heralding the rebirth that was about to begin.

Through hypnotic regression, I knew that during the breakdown I'd experienced a moment of trauma. I knew that a piece of me was frozen in time and space. Using my imagination, I saw myself in that frozen memory as Captain Marvel and the survival urge of trauma as electricity surging through me. The trauma energy could finally ground down into the earth, completing its journey.

Prepared in the psychic realm, it was time for the physical trauma release.

Surrendering to my body's wisdom, I let the frozen trauma energy have more space and trusted my body to shake it off. Powerful survival energy that my poor confused psyche had believed I needed to stay alive in a moment of intense inner shaming. In that deluded state of sleeplessness and stress, I'd come to believe that I was controlled subtly by the devil. A deep, dark secret I carried for years. Not that I was really continuing to believe the devil himself controlled me, but I continued to be ashamed that I'd believed such delusion. A spiritual awakening, yes, but also a deep sense of shame and fear of rejection. The devil is the classic symbol of the church for shaming powerful, spiritual women who don't fit the compliant, virginal mother role.

Once the survival energy had passed through, the part of me wanting external things to be seen as successful disappeared. The allure of the online law of attraction lifestyle went with it and I wanted to distance myself from that "make 6 or 7 figures" marketing machine. All of these costly mistakes and the intense inner and outer criticism were coming from the deep wound and the self-protection mechanisms my mind created around it.

With the trauma energy gone, I thought that was it. Life and the book would flow but an experience like that leaves a lot of damage. I was only beginning to find and understand the shattered pieces it had revealed inside.

Over the next two years, more precise healing tools came to me to uncover more lost, buried pieces of who I am. More importantly, to understand the bigger context of how they got lost and buried along the way so I could empower others with the same kind of self-awareness. Each recovered piece, in both myself and my clients, deepening my compassion for human suffering and bringing a ray of hope that peace is possible.

When there's a strong enough love to heal the deepest wound and tell the truth of the pieces lost in the darkness, grace can flow and take care of peace.

JACQUI MCGINN

Jacqui is an energy healer, hypnotherapist, and Japanese teacher based in the South of England. While living in Japan, she experienced a breakdown that began her healing career and inspired her to share her lived experience in a solo book "Pieces to Peace".

Jacqui's combined training in energy healing modalities and hypnotherapy has enabled her to create a unique practice that holds a compassionate space for deeper healing. Jacqui believes that expressing the heart's truth in a safe space brings lost, buried, and broken pieces of us back together. Just like the Japanese art of kintsugi mends broken pottery pieces with gold lacquer and creates unique and beautiful art.

Jacqui also works as a freelance Japanese teacher for teenagers who love the language and culture, and who want to go to Japan someday.

Watch out for Jacqui's book "Pieces to Peace":
https://jacquimcginn.com/pieces-to-peace-book
Website: https://jacquimcginn.com
Instagram: https://www.instagram.com/jacqui_mcginn/

10

HANNAH GAIR

KNOW YOUR VALUE

*B*usiness. It's such a glamorous word or is it? I have been asked to write from a slightly different angle for my contribution. Not the typical approach one would expect when picking up a book related to business, but without my topic, well you won't get far, as underneath your exciting vision, the business model, the marketing strategies, the KPI's and sales, is an underlying element that we as women absolutely need to harness, accept and adopt into our own personal life. A word that is thrown around on social media and in podcasts, yet can be one of the most difficult things for us to grab a hold of wholeheartedly and foster personally.

It's something that may have been bruised and knocked about over the years, like wild waves crashing upon a rock, slowly eroding and eating this part of us away.

Many contributing factors can be taken into consideration for what I am about to speak about. Our internal thoughts being one, where we have believed that we don't measure up, the deadly comparison game being played where we look outwardly at other women, believing they are superior to us as individuals (this can be multifaceted), which results in us allowing our thoughts to spiral and spiralling thoughts (should we allow them) dictate our thinking where toxic thoughts find a breeding ground. This in turn leads us to an unhealthy mindset where our self-perception is distorted and filled with lies.

Ever felt like you're not good enough?

Or maybe you have had unrealistic expectations placed on you, external voices fighting to dictate your life while controlling your steering wheel and you find yourself southbound, going in the wrong direction, wanting so desperately to head north, but don't have the ability to turn your own steering wheel around, so there you are, slowly suffocating for the sake of someone else, while living a half-empty life.

Or maybe you have had harsh opinions spoken over your life, unwelcome comments and judgement sprayed over your character with misinformation and judgement and there you stand deflated and lost, while adopting these opinions as truth, yet deep within, you are a stranger to yourself, living a life that is not your own, costing you your potential and living the best version of yourself.

Well, girl, it's time to move on, to abandon the opinions, to restore the lies with truth, to hang up your mask, to posture yourself with assertiveness, to put your armour on and live a life that is filled with the golden word!

Value.

"The regard that something is held to deserve; the importance, worth, or usefulness of something"

Did you catch that? Read it again, more slowly this time.

I will come back to that, to you, to us, but thought I would share a story where my value on many levels was challenged in the corporate world.

Enter the boardroom with me. A mother of three in her mid-thirties , who could change a diaper with her eyes closed, handle toddlers and sleepless nights like a boss, but was learning the art of working in a Boys Club and asserting herself. The scenario which won't be dramatised or minimised is this;

Hannah (me) swallows hard and asks for a meeting with the Managing Director, General Manager and National Sales Manager. I could see that there was an unfair allocation towards me, compared to the other male Business Development Managers within the organisation, whereby the other BDM's were getting all the large accountants deemed as 'whales' allocated to them. The large deal flows, the easier sales if you like. I had previously been asked by management, to take my accounts to strip bars and to get drunk with them and upon me asking the reason, it was said rather dismissively, that it would make a good story within the industry (a pastor's wife at the time) entertaining men in that environment. It became apparent without any spoken words, that the reason for me not getting the larger accountants was due to my own values. I stood my ground and wouldn't comply with the requests until this meeting that you and I are currently sitting in (big mistake- don't ever compromise your ethics!)

Ok... Back in the boardroom, where I could feel myself acting more confident than I felt. The meeting had commenced and I put my request in to have larger clients allocated to me. I stated the unfairness of what was transpiring within the team and it was my turn, and gulp... I would take the clients to the bar. The male management all shook their heads yes in agreement and I would be set up for meetings the following week when I was required to fly interstate. While on the plane, I was thinking of ways to control the 'drinking' situation while fulfilling my role professionally, as there were safety concerns of which we women need to be mindful.

Bingo! The hotel that I was staying at had a bar downstairs and I would make arrangements with the new account (two male Managing Directors) to meet me there. I'd be safe right?

The late afternoon meeting in the lobby bar had commenced and I was ordering the drinks with one of the managing directors standing next to me. I got a vibe off him but made sure I held my shoulders back and was confident. The drinks were poured and I simply said to the bartender to charge my room which was 321 (didn't give it thought) as opposed to signing for it. One drink down and I could see these boys were still thirsty. I politely sipped my apple cider, not wanting it to go to my head. I then asked obligingly if they would like another beer? To which they said yes. Lucky for me they were smokers, so they went outside to have their nicotine hit, while I took my drink back to the bar, asked the bartender to pour ¾ of it down the sink, so I didn't have to finish it, ordered the two extra drinks and then waited for my 'meeting' to recommence.

The second drink was consumed and a third was requested. It just happened to be a friend's opening night for her new business and she was having an industry party down the road at the local pub, which I was to later attend. I was feeling a little uneasy but kept telling myself that drinking with men, who wanted to get drunk with a 'pretty' lady, was part of the deal.

Instead of staying on-site, I suggested we go to this local pub, so at least these guys were out of my hotel and I would be at the same venue with someone I knew.

So there we were, now at the local pub where the account I was trying to win, were on their third drink and settling in for the evening. I made eye contact with my friend who casually came over and innocently asked if we all wanted to join her party? I could have killed her. My lack of assertiveness and not knowing how to steer the conversation differently to shut the idea down came into play and both the men immediately jumped at the opportunity.

Fast forward a few hours, the party is a little loose and in full swing. I'm sipping water, uptight but smiling, wanting to celebrate my friend and still getting the same bad vibe from the managing director as earlier before. His alcohol consumption, clearly in full effect, led him to make sexual comments towards me. I smiled awkwardly while being internally horrified by his language and suggestions, but again, didn't know how to handle the situation at the time. My friend who was hosting the party could now see I was feeling uncomfortable and was my strength. She called a cab and walked me to it, closed the door after I hopped in and told me to text her when I was in my room safely. Unbeknownst to me, she kicked the managing directors out, once I left and that was that.

When I got back to my hotel, I had a 'yucky' feeling inside (especially after the sexual comments made towards me). I texted my employer due to the time and said I didn't want this account and elaborated on what had happened, thinking he would have a Duty of Care and even some sort of compassion. At that stage, I didn't care what the ramifications were going to be professionally, I just wasn't going to see these two men again. I received a response to my text, which I felt was disturbing. "Don't worry", I read, "we can use this situation to get more deals out of this guy." I literally gasped, put on my pj's and crawled into bed feeling deflated and disrespected. That's when my phone began to ring constantly by the man who was trying his luck on me, followed by a barrage of sexual text messages which came streaming in. I ignored it all and told myself that I would be safe as I was in a hotel room. Roughly thirty minutes later, I heard someone trying to break into my room and calling my name. I laid there in the dark, stunned with fear. My arms felt like led, I slowly lifted them, trying not to make a sound to reach for the hotel phone to call for help. The voice outside my door was that of the managing director from whom I had gotten the bad vibe. His shoulder was now pounding the door, bang, bang, bang as he was trying to break into my room with force. I launched out of bed, grabbed my mobile phone and cowered in the corner crying and frightened. My reaction (who knows why) was to text my managing director asking for help. What was he going to do 1200 kilometres away? He texted me back and coached me through what seemed to be a long amount of time, telling me to be quiet and not move.

Eventually, the door handle was released and the banging subsided. A few minutes later, I had the urge to peer out my hotel window which overlooked the car park. In the darkness, I saw the man trying to break into my room, reverse his white Range Rover and drive away. I was a mess and crying in the darkness. I rang reception and told them what had just occurred and asked to be moved to a new room. I laid awake all night in fear.

The following morning, I drove to the airport and called my dad along the way. He answered and my voice cracked due to emotion. I remember saying to Dad in that conversation, how hard it is for a woman to work in a man's world. Dad listened and was obviously very angry at what had occurred and gave me the courage to stand up for myself and to take the steps that I needed to take.

Unfortunately, I felt the situation was mishandled by management and I ended up resigning from my position. It was minimised and I felt disrespected and devalued. I had to follow up the matter privately to resolve how in the world a man got to my door in a hotel that has security? When I got to the bottom of it, I was flabbergasted by how audacious he was.

I am aware that many women in the working world have been sexualised due to their gender. You only have to sit at a round table, with other women to hear their horror stories and the way it has made them feel, which is why it's vital that we intrinsically understand who we are and the value we hold as women, as people, as business owners!

Without having a deep understanding, we inhibit ourselves from flourishing and becoming all we have been created for, it silences us when words need to be spoken or action undertaken, it prevents us from actively living out our dreams and stepping into the unknown with courage.

So let's look at some of the signs that manifest when we lack self-confidence and value.

According to the 69 most common signs of low self-worth, the following points outline that you may have this.

- You have problems loving and accepting yourself the way you are.
- You criticise and judge yourself regularly.
- You expect perfection from yourself at all times.
- You wish you could look like or be like someone else.
- You struggle with social interactions and often feel overlooked and ignored in conversations.
- You exaggerate to appear more interesting when talking to others.
- You are easily embarrassed in conversations because you don't feel important or intelligent enough to contribute something useful.
- You feel ashamed of yourself.
- You feel uncomfortable with too much attention.
- You are unsure how to react to praise.
- You struggle financially because, deep down, you feel you don't deserve an abundant, worry-free life.
- You feel awkward asking for what you deserve or charging appropriately for your services.
- OR You don't believe in yourself and distrust your abilities which lead to;
- You value other people's views and opinions more than your own because you consider them more important than yours.
- You have difficulty making decisions and ask everybody you know what they would do in your situation instead of listening to your intuition.

- You only believe that your point of view is legitimate if other people agree with you.
- You always worry about the potential consequences of your choices and decisions.
- You often feel (or are) victimised or bullied.
- You tend to procrastinate because, deep inside, you feel that once you start you will fail.
- You suffer from crippling self-doubt.
- You worry that all things you start are automatically destined to fail.
- You consider yourself an under-achiever compared to others.
- You always expect the worst so you won't be disappointed when you don't succeed.
- You suffer from anxiety in daily life and unfamiliar situations.
- You fear change.
- You regularly agonise about the future.
- You avoid situations that take you out of your comfort zone.
- You tend to abandon your dreams for fear that you don't have what it takes to succeed.

Do any of the above points sound familiar to you or feel hard-hitting?

If so, let's continue to fight like girls and keep on this road of self-discovery, by arming yourself with tools to begin the process of boosting your self-esteem and self-worth. In order to do that, you need to take steps (can I say, that taking these steps, a step, is the beginning of you commencing your journey to value).

Sometimes we need to go back in order to move forward. What I mean by that is, we are required to do some digging of our past (and I mean deep digging) to understand where and how our misconception of self-perception was formed. To find the root by identifying where and when, we began to lose the ability in knowing our value. This is where counselling comes into play. Sitting with a professional who can safely unpack your past to make sense of it, harmful patterns of thinking are gently corrected, so the lens in how you view yourself becomes balanced and healthy.

A healthy understanding of who you are, is the beginning of building up your self-worth.

There may be people in your life who are toxic and stumping your growth, and hindering your self-esteem. Implementing boundaries to those voices/people may be a difficult step, however, unless you rid yourself of those harsh opinions, then you are going to be enslaved to them and stuck.

Are there any people in your life, who disable you from not only attaining your goals and dreams but are disrespectful and bring emotional harm your way? Sometimes this can be passive-aggressive, subtle, other times it's glaringly obvious. If so, I urge you to suck in courage and place safe perimeters around yourself. Let go of guilt and allow that to be replaced with self-worth, as destructive people bring destructive energy.

It's time to unearth your potential and begin living in a place where decisions you make reflect the way you see yourself or want to see your future self and that, my friend, should be brimming with value.

It may be uncomfortable and strange to begin with, however as you grow in self-love, your perception of who you are and the world around you shifts in a beautiful way. You begin moving in a direction that manifests goodness, opportunity, healthy relationships and yes a business built on a strong foundation. We all know that a strong foundation produces growth, longevity and abundance.

YOU hold the power within, to make healthy decisions and to go on the hunt for further self-discovery, which when conducted healthily, leads to self-love, which couples itself with the way we value ourselves.

This is your prompting, your quiet moment for any needed change and with change comes choice. You have the ability to choose where your life leads, the path you will travel and the people you will have on your journey. You, my friend, are your own key.

References:

The 69 most common signs of low self-worth - The Self-Worth Experiment (increasingselfworth.com)

HANNAH GAIR

Hannah has the privilege of raising three beautiful children (one with special needs) as a single mum and counts it an absolute blessing – she calls motherhood a beautiful mess. Hannah is passionate about educating, equipping and empowering women on a holistic basis, with the intent that each individual reaches her full potential with boldness. Hannah owns multiple businesses which keep her busy and is always on the lookout for her next investment opportunity. Hannah is a published author, worked as a TV presenter and model, spoke at conferences nationally and internationally, written for numerous women's magazines and blogs globally, but most importantly, is utterly passionate towards life and the gift it brings every single day. Hannah has a heart to always live it large and wholly, while never forgetting to show kindness along the way.

Empire Lane Advisory | Investment property - Your Lane to Success
Website: www.empirelaneadvisory.com.au/
Facebook: Hannah Gair
Instagram: @empirelaneadvisory

11

MICHELE DICKINSON

A SIXTH SENSE: THE CALL OF THE SOUL

I met my soul today. Her eyes were kind, her smile warm, and she invited me in with a radiance that shone so bright. Without uttering a single word, I felt safe in her presence. She held out her hand and I accepted it in mine. I felt her. I know her. I am her.

Throughout my life, I've sensed an ancient, inner wisdom within. An unfamiliar voice and sensation in my body. A whisper calling to me.

"Sensed?", you ask? Yes, but not in the traditional meaning of the word. My internal experience did not originate from an external stimulus. This was something primal laying dormant inside of me - waiting patiently to be unleashed.

A more aligned description would be: "a keen intuitive awareness of or sensitivity to the presence or importance of something." In my own words? A deep-rooted knowing that I'm here for a very specific purpose; to share a very specific message. Distilled even further? A sixth sense. A gut feeling. As I know her today, she is the whisper of my soul.

In my experience, one does not just speak their truth. It is a process you must move through, which I believe happens in three stages of embodying your intuition until life is given to your internal "knowing" and words are birthed and spoken.

Your only job is to awaken, accept, and surrender to the whispers of your soul.

AWAKENING TO YOUR TRUTH: THE WELCOMING

Oh, dear girl. All you ever wanted was to be loved and accepted. You were timid and unsure, words resting on your heart with bated breath, but never spoken aloud. Your quiet, sensitive nature, misunderstood and mocked. They didn't know how their words broke you. And you didn't know the only love and acceptance you needed was your own.

Awakening to your truth is to know thyself, but there were times I didn't.

My teenage years were rough. I felt lost, sad, disconnected and closed off.

Everyone talks about high school as being the best time of their life, but for me, it most certainly wasn't.

It was lonely. I was lonely.

Actually, I hated myself! I hated my naturally curly, red hair. I hated my freckles. I hated that I didn't have a boyfriend like everyone else in school. I hated my body. I deprived myself of food so I could be thin. I was a follower so I wouldn't stand out like a sore thumb and draw attention to myself. I "hated" my parents for being so strict and feeling like I had no sense of fun, freedom or privacy.

I hated life and dimmed my light.

Looking back on those four years, one experience stands out in my mind the most and it is when my healing process and journey home to myself began.

Before I go on, it's important to note that while I was raised a Catholic and attended 12 years of Catholic schooling, I never felt connected to the Church and all of its ridiculous rules about who will go to Heaven or Hell. Did I believe in God, Jesus, and the Holy Spirit? Yes!

More so, I believed in the concept of a higher power.

It was Junior year. I was in my ridiculously good looking religion teacher's class when we were presented with an opportunity to attend a so-called "life-changing" spiritual retreat.

The invitation was extended to us if we felt "called" to participate. "CALLED?", I thought as I sat wondering what this feeling was in my belly.

I had no idea what they were talking about, but couldn't deny this feeling that I was meant to be there. And so the journey began.

When I arrived at the retreat, I settled into my room, which seemed more like solitary confinement, and then headed to the gathering room where I was given instructions for what to expect.

The daytime activities didn't scare me much, but the final activity of the night made me anxious.

We'd be sitting in "circle" with everyone, passing around a candle to share anything in our hearts if we felt "called".

There was definitely a message inside of me that wanted to be expressed, but I had no idea how to put that into words.

And so that first night, as a group of about 25 of us sat in a circle, I remained silent and watched as a handful of people accepted the flickering candle and spoke the truth(s) of their soul.

It was an emotional night, to say the least and I was both eager and happy to go to bed.

Saturday morning rolled around with a full day of activities.

One of which was writing a personal message to "friends" at the retreat. I received many, but one stood out among the others. It was from a very kind girl named Jasmine and her words will live with me forever. She wrote: "You have a quiet voice, but a loud spirit." My interpretation of that: it doesn't matter how loud your voice is, but rather, it is the energy and intention behind your words that carries the power and vibrational potency that makes a difference in the hearts and minds of others.

The self-discovery work was intense, which I'd never done before. It wasn't easy, but something about it felt right and I now realize the more you peel back your layers and get to the core of who you are, the stronger your intuition and truth become.

In essence, the channel through which she flows becomes clearer the more you know yourself. You can think of it this way: if you were travelling through the jungle, there wouldn't necessarily be a clear path, you'd need a sharp tool to clear the brush in front of you in order to forge ahead.

The same goes for your intuition - there must be an unobstructed path for her to travel and your intuition cannot come through until your healing journey has been activated.

This process was activated for me the last night at the retreat when I finally let my guard down and shared the truth laying on my heart.

The weight of my anxiety was building in my chest - although I had a desire to speak, I didn't know what to say and the fear of judgement terrified me.

But not speaking also terrified me, so I nervously grabbed the candle and returned to my place in the circle.

I uttered my first words: "I honestly have no idea what I'm going to say right now. I don't have a deep story to tell of how my parents abused me or how my brother died of a heroin overdose, so I'm just going to talk and whatever comes out, comes out, because if I don't put into words what I'm feeling inside right now, I'll regret it for the rest of my life."

And so I began. I don't remember what I said exactly, but it went something like...

"We are all different AND we are all perfectly unique. It's okay if you haven't fully accepted who you are deep down because you're still beautiful on the inside. It's okay if you don't fully know who the hell you are. It's okay to be scared and unsure of yourself. It's okay if you're figuring it all out as you place one foot in front of the other. It's okay to make mistakes and fuck it all up as you try." My most important message was that we all have a voice and if you feel compelled to speak your truth you must!

I didn't know at the time I was speaking mine and I believe I healed myself a little bit at that moment.

There was a deep sense of joy and peace that resonated throughout my entire being and I could truly see myself now, and the light that lived within me.

It was an awakening - one of those experiences that changes you on the inside. I'd never look at life the same again and I was ready to integrate my learnings back into my everyday life.

I learned that anything external doesn't matter because, at my core, I knew I was pure love, and that energy felt safe. Every time I'd return to that core essence, I not only felt love for myself, but for those around me, and even extending beyond that, the world.

In what way can you let your light shine a little brighter today and share your truth with someone?

ACCEPTING YOUR TRUTH: THE HEALING

I'm starting to see

That it's all up to me

To be as free as I want to be

Walls broken down

Limits of time unfound

The masks are falling

My truth is calling

It's ringing loud and clear

There's nothing left to fear

I'm here to share and serve

After I returned home from my spiritual retreat, I had good intentions of remaining the "holy roller" I had now claimed myself to be. But sustaining that new identity proved challenging when I was back in my everyday environment.

Between high school and my late 20s, my life wasn't very intentional, kind of like a leaf on a windy day with no direction - I just landed wherever.

I knew I didn't want to go to college, but my parents insisted.

There was something telling me not to go - that college wasn't my path - but when my parents asked what else I wanted to do, I didn't have a great answer.

All I remember saying was: "I just want to do something creative."

That clearly was a less than acceptable response because off to college I went.

I studied accounting, which in my opinion, was a form of slow torture, but I did it anyway because I was good at it and hoped I'd make a lot of money.

After four long years, I graduated from college and landed myself a stable job at one of the world's largest investment management companies.

16 years went by as I climbed my way up the corporate ladder. Some might say I had it all: a six-figure salary, Masters Degree in Tax & Financial Planning, a hands-on husband and healthy children.

But I felt so empty inside and nothing seemed to fill the growing void. It was a defining moment and I knew I was being pulled towards something bigger than myself.

All the boxes were checked for a happy and fulfilled life, yet: I felt empty inside, I didn't know who I was outside of all my titles. I had zero clue what I truly wanted in a career, and I was asking myself all the existential questions.

It was frustrating because I just wanted someone to give me all the answers.

Like, "Hey Michele, here's exactly what you were created for. This is your purpose. Now, go forth and change lives!"

Ah, if only life were that simple.

Nothing prepares you for these experiences. You have to be willing to do the work on yourself to figure it out and move through what feels like a heavy pile of stinky shit.

I knew I was being called to redefine myself, my passions and my purpose, and that's when everything changed because I realized I had two choices:

1. Continue playing life by someone else's rules and look back with regret because of dreams I left unfulfilled.
2. Explore the "whisper" telling me I was made to do bigger things in life and trust that path would lead me somewhere I was meant to be.

It was time to go inward and I welcomed the invitation. If you've ever moved through a spiritual awakening, then you know it's not all butterflies and rainbows.

This was deep, expansive work - exploring myself in ways I never had before. But by doing so, I was able to discern where I was honoring my truth and where I was lying to myself.

The byproduct of that inner work? I could see the parts of me I liked and where I was still rejecting myself. I faced the parts of me I disliked and I asked them what they needed. Healing? Forgiveness? Love? Compassion? Understanding?

It wasn't easy, but the more attention I gave the parts of me I thought were broken and made me ache inside, the more I healed and the more beautiful I became....to myself.

That was a 12 month journey of self-inquiry, self-discovery and healing and the more I explored my inner landscape, the more I awakened to the truth that was there all along.

When you're in the early stages of connecting with and channelling your intuition, it's easier to tap into her when you're in an environment that allows you to thrive intuitively.

Practically speaking, you might be wondering what that looks like:

- Make time for daily rituals that allow you to practice mindfulness and introspection. My favorite daily practice is meditation.
- Practice thought and belief work. Byron Katie's method, The Work, is life changing.
- Trust yourself to make decisions that are best for you and align with what you value. This means, avoid seeking external approval and/or validation out of fear you'll make a "wrong" decision.

SPEAKING YOUR TRUTH: THE LIBERATION

There is a wild woman rising inside of me longing to be set free. Her energy is primal & raw, with wild like fire in her heart and truth in her eyes. I hear and heed her call. She is liberated and venerated.

After 12 months of self-inquiry and what I now call "Soul Discovery™", I received my rite of passage and was ready to take the next step on my journey of personal evolution.

My spiritual awakening happened one year before I gave birth to my third and final baby, Brayden, and everything came to a head while I was home with him on maternity leave.

While I was happy in most areas of my life, my work still felt misaligned. I thought to myself, "if not Corporate America, then what?"

During this time, I was broadening (and deepening) my understanding of spirituality and was on a mission to discover my life's purpose, more specifically, my Dharma.

Ironically, I found exactly what I was looking for when I stumbled upon a podcast promoting an online group coaching program called Doshas & Dharma: A 5 Week Journey to Discovering Your Life's Purpose.

I took this as a sign, and knew I had to join - it was the catalyst of my entrepreneurial journey.

The program was amazing because I had no idea what I was passionate about or good at outside of my corporate job and it helped me discover my passions and gifts, which I wanted to use to help others.

It became clear that Life Coaching was my path. I was scared, but I took the leap and launched my coaching business while working full-time at my 9-5.

Holy smokes, the learning curve was steep and it felt challenging putting myself out there as someone who was (and still is) healing deep childhood wounds and has a massive fear of rejection.

I'll be the first to admit, growth is uncomfortable. But a crucial element of transformation and healing is embracing and accepting your imperfections, speaking your truth and letting yourself be seen.

After launching my Life Coaching business while on maternity leave, I returned back to my 9-5. I won't lie, it was a juggle that took a toll on me mentally, emotionally, and physically, but I couldn't give up on my purpose, so something had to change.

Once again, I came to a fork in the road and here's why...

While striving to climb the corporate ladder, I had lost sight of interests and hobbies that used to spark curiosity, creativity, and joy. I was operating heavily out of masculine energy and I could sense this in my body. My anxiety was at an all-time high, feeling irritable and exhausted.

This escalated to the point where the entire right side of my body was numb, but all the MRIs and EKGs (not fun! Go Google it.) came back normal and the doctors didn't have any answers for what was happening to me.

So, I decided to take a short-term leave (six weeks) from my corporate job with a 50% pay cut. I knew it was going to be tight, but I didn't see any other choice.

I took this time to really pull back and focus solely on what mattered most to me - my family, my coaching business, and my wellbeing.

If you've ever done a "my best day" visualization, this was me living mine.

About the second week into my leave, I learned a freakishly interesting fact that I believe explains the numbness I was experiencing...

The left side of your brain (the masculine side) controls the right side of your body. "It is the part of us that is assertive, logical, analytical, doing, controlling, aggressive, rushing, always pushing us to survive, and has its origin in our minds. The right side of your brain controls the left side of your body - your feminine side - which is all about the emotional, feeling, subjective, musical, spatial perception, pieces together in ricochet fashion, abstract, intuitive approach and the being, receiving, relational sides of ourselves."

The way I interpret this is: my 9-5, which I was resisting hardcore, entailed more left-brained work and was controlling the right side of my body. Hence, the numbness because the left side of my brain was in overdrive.

So, it's no coincidence to me that the week after I was on leave, the numbness had dissipated. I was focusing more time and energy into my life coaching business- a more creative outlet that I actually enjoyed and found my purposeful expression in.

All this to say, your body and soul speak to you and guide you. Take time to tune in and listen to what they have to say.

While I've come a long way - leaning more and more into my intuition and truth - this is a lifelong process.

It's not easy and it requires commitment to your personal evolution, and growth day in and day out.

But I "see" now, there really isn't any other way to be.

MICHELE DICKINSON

Michele Dickinson is an Intuitive Life Coach who lives in Pennsylvania with her husband and three kiddos. She guides high-achieving women to rediscover themselves, align to their deeper purpose through their work, and birth their creative ideas through heart-centered businesses. Michele created the proprietary Passion to Purpose Success Method™ and uses this in her 1:1 coaching experience, Intuitive Pursuit of Passion™.

Michele found her passion and "calling" for coaching after a spiritual awakening. Before that, she spent 16 years as a Corporate leader holding a Bachelor's degree in Business and Master's degree in Taxation and Financial Planning.

In her spare time Michele enjoys yoga, meditation, pulling tarot, poetry, and surrounding herself with anyone who cracks a good joke.

If you'd like to learn how to rediscover yourself, reignite your passion, and reinvent your life & career, connect with Michele on Instagram and inside her private Facebook™ community.

www.facebook.com/michele.dickinson.963
www.facebook.com/groups/workingmomswantingmore
www.instagram.com/the_michele_dickinson/

12

BRANKA PESTAR HAJŠEK

BEING HUMAN

I was a curious and brave girl, but the world convinced me that this is a bad thing. "Just be beautiful and find a husband, was the message I received." People don't like loud girls, girls with opinions and difficult questions. Just be like the rest and be happy if anyone wants you." I felt that there was so much more to this life. And I was right, but it was my story to write.

I couldn't be the good girl everyone expected, I felt different from the start, but at that time I didn't know all I know now. You are reading my journey from the love to the pain, from the joy to the guilt and shame, having fallen in a deep darkness to find a way back to peace, love, power and freedom.

So, let me walk you through my lows and highs, because I believe you can find parts of you within it. After all, we have so much in common, starting with being human.

WHO IS SHE?

Many asked while I lived my wild-life and followed my truth. The answers were wide and the labels oftens judgemental. I did it anyway, followed my voice and made it a voice for many. This was too much for people to understand and that hurts sometimes, when you are an empath. At some point, it was even too much for me to handle, so I closed my heart a bit, (but not completely). I just learned how to survive in this world. Overtime it accumulated many layers of anger, guilt, shame and misery, until finally, as grown women, I realised how to set myself free and connect with my heart again.

As with every life story, it all starts in a family, where life is created. No matter how hard we want to fight it, our relative's roots are connected to our life and impact us. So here I was, in a middle of a big working-class family, living in a catholic village, trying to make a family work and look good. It was important to look good on the outside. Many things were important just because this was how it has always been, I was told. This was hard to understand, why bother if you do not feel it?

I ran barefoot, danced in a rain, learned how to make a fire and break wood. I saw people behind the roles, gender and positions, and asked questions many adults never did. But I wanted to know, so I asked anyway, but in return the responses were crushing my wings;

"That's how the world works."

"This is how we do it."

"You wouldn't understand."

"What kind of stupid, naive question is that?"

These were the lines that usually came, when I didn't accept some childish answers that made me look like a dummy. I was young, too young for the questions I know, but serious when I asked. This was real for me, but yet, I was left alone with it. Questions made people uncomfortable, I saw through the reactions to what I said. While observing, I created a belief that I hurt them. Not knowing I just touched their pain which was already there. I felt guilty all of the time growing up, missing the fact that everyone carries his own guilt and responsibility. When you take it on yourself, it does not mean it is all you, it just means you are aware of your part in it.

I demanded attention, but there wasn't a time for that, there was plenty of work inside and outside the house. So I lived in the middle and observed around. The love I received was usually connected with me being a good girl, doing the right thing and felt absent, when I made a mistake or did something out of the ordinary. This is how most of us were raised, I learned later. I was the wild one, had fun and walked around in the middle of the night. Moved back and forth with my mom and sisters, looking for someone to be with but somehow I didn't let anyone near me. I saw many things, but I knew a limit I didn't pass and somehow managed to stay safe and true to myself. I had support and trust from my parents, and the choice to live in my own way and be responsible for my actions. Many things I had, yet many things I missed. Now, feeling deep gratitude since I know how deep my roots go and what was necessary for my parents and grandparents to survive. Patterns are so deeply rooted in our brain and we see the reflection of it in families, cultures, religions, public systems and businesses...

EMOTIONAL CONFUSION

I was called stubborn every time I expressed my feelings. There was fear, sadness, anger and misery, but it was all combined into a state of rebellion. No wonder my response as a teenager was all about anger. I was like a firebomb, exploding every time I felt something unpleasant. I didn't know how to express it properly, so I did the best I could.

Just like most of us, I developed a view of not being enough. Felt unheard, unseen, and many times, misunderstood. There was guilt and shame for every mistake and I was left alone with these big feelings. Every time I wanted to express myself, I was a rebel. Every time I did what was expected, I was a good girl. But I observed the good girls in adult life and saw their cages and felt the pain surrounding them. Buried so deep in their body, that they were convinced they act out of love. Not realizing that this is the only way they ever felt loved, accepted and valued. Is this really everything we can have in this life? Is this really all there is to live for?

The more years passed, the more I saw and heard about life. It was perceived as hard, painful and conditioned. I always questioned why? Why do some people have it all, and others don't? Why do people change behaviour? Why is there so much pressure on labels and titles? Why is there such a big difference between women and men?

LIFE IS GOOD

I was living a life, had a crowd of people I would spend time and party with, and close friends to share secrets and life questions. In a search to find my way, I bounced from being girly and appealing to being in a state of "f#*k off", wearing boys' clothes to present in my own style. Then, I met a man. We were so different but it seemed like this was the glue for our connection. We were good friends, who didn't let themselves believe, they fell in love. I was so afraid to be loved I refused every act of love and kindness toward me, just to keep me safe. But this man slowly made it through my walls of insecurity and fear, he made sure my nature was beautiful. He was the man I dreamed about, strong, thoughtful, and caring, prepared to listen to me and not afraid of my wild nature. We don't have a date of the start, but we do have the passion to be together.

SEEING NEW POSSIBILITIES

Looking at life, it was almost all messed up in my view and it felt like I was the only one who even noticed it. When I discovered economy and psychology in high school, I saw the background of my observations. I understood systems and mechanisms that run life. I felt a strong urge to find a way to change things for the better. I saw many people being miserable at their jobs and questioned, is that really necessary? I believed in a better world, and now I had answers to dream about it more realistically.

"What do you see in economy?" many asked me, as they saw my wild nature and big perspective on life.

"I found missing answers to my questions. I found possibilities not taken. I saw the opportunity to make a world a better place." I said, as I absorbed a new layer of understanding to this world.

It was the opposite perspective to what was mostly observed, but it provided many benefits for all actors in the game, it would make owners and stakeholders happy with profits, governments get taxes, leaders and directors would be pleased, employees felt valued enough to do the best they can, while also accumulating great benefit to the families of everyone involved.

The reality was quite the opposite, and when I expressed my view, there was usually resistance on the other side. But I saw evidences in real life and I am still optimistic, but now I know that not everyone is prepared to hear my truth – yet.

PAIN CHANGES PEOPLE

And then, the big change came into my life. I meet chronic pain when I was 18 years old, received a diagnosis 'fast' only because I didn't give up. Again it has been proven to me, that speaking your truth is important. Endometriosis changed my life plans and ambitions, isolated me from people I knew and hung out with. It made me look at life and myself from a different angle. I dived deep into the condition, sharing information and supported women with the same condition, worked as a volunteer for eight years to share awareness and support. We talked basics since there was so much hidden. But there also was pain that nobody talked about, so much guilt and shame is thrown at women, who find themselves in pain. Many times I was called crazy, sensitive or lazy in some form, just because I didn't find a release from the pain. Doctors should've be there to help me, but when you meet a disease so unknown and stigmatised, it was a lesson for me, to follow my body and my truth, to find my own answers. So I did, while empowering other endo-sisters to stand up for themselves and seek diagnosis after years of humiliation and ignorance. It was hard to see the reality of the world, but it has made me stronger. This pain put me on the path of my own emotional empowerment.

BIG REALISATION

That moment I realized my message was not meant for the people that could not hear. "There is more to this life, than suffering. I need to find people and places where people believe in possibilities." I understood that it does not matter if people around me can't hear it. I hear this melody clearly and I will follow it no matter what.

So there I was, from the large crowd of people around me, only three would believe me and stood close by my side on this "endo" journey. It was hard to accept, but I had life to handle and pain to overcome. I had to face my fears and find a way out of this mess. Pain and the inability to attend university I loved, combined with other fights, made me depressed and anxious. I fell in deep darkness but soon realized only myself could climb out of it. While people admired me for my strength, I felt powerless. Soon after, I started to explore the deep ocean of emotions we all poses. I realised, how fucked up our view on emotions is, how we deny the intelligence they bring to us and what it actually means to be human.

It became clear why I felt strange when listened to positive mindset methods. I saw that they can drive you, in a way, to delete or deny unpleasant emotions. More also, why it felt wrong when people would look for help, receive a ton of guilt for not making this or that, or decided that they did not want to change. It is bigger than this, I believed, and slowly I uncovered the secrets of human behaviour and design.

FROM DARKNESS TO THE LIGHT

I started to understand, why people would look away from my questions. I was not wrong to say it, but it was too much for the other person. People are in survival mode most of their life, working and acting the best they can, according to their level of consciousness and ignorance. Learning the main difference between surviving and living I decided, "I do not want just survive this life, I want to live!"

I dived deep into the body first, wanted to feel healthy again, but realised I was drowning in guilt, shame and pain. Every part of my life was now connected to this darkness and I didn't know myself anymore. I was just a shadow of the women I once was. And this made me connect the dots and started to look at all aspects, emotion, mind and body.

The first big light sparkled when a pregnancy test finally came up positive. The decision we made as parents, to change some patterns from our family, made us more self-aware and put us on a new path of self-realisation. Many things happened and struggles appeared, but we stood strong in our love and decided to make it work together through the storm. It was a time for a second big lesson; it all comes from inside ourselves, people and circumstances are just helping revealing our inner state. Nothing from the outside can give us love and care if we are not prepared to accept and feel it.

Now there was a shock – Why do we doing this to ourselves? "I was hurt and this was my way of surviving", I realised. But right there lies a pearl of big wisdom "I have the power to make myself smile again, feel life and joy."

I started to discover human experience, learning about survival mechanisms and saw how afraid and ashamed I felt most of my life. On the outside standing strong, but deep inside I absorbed every judgment, blame and shame as a real fact.

It was time to make a change, to let go of the persona that was conditioned to a belief that causes us to suffer in life. No matter the storms, my centre was always here with me, supporting my steps, mistakes and wins. All the pains made me stronger and every mistake held wisdom in it.

I knew that every emotion is there for a reason. As they were ignored and misunderstood most of my life, strong reactions were screams from the heart. My reactive and aggressive mind were defending me from getting burned again. I was living from the past, afraid about the future.

I found techniques to release these trapped feelings and made a commitment to feel joy every day. I started to encourage myself and my body to do it, to try, to believe. Was dedicated to gain new experiences and embody the feelings of happiness, gratitude and joy I had forgoten about. This was hard work, as I had stong analitical mind and had to overcome it, to make a lasting change.

But then, I wanted to clear everything there is, to be like the stories we hear about those perfect people, happy all the time. The feeling of not being there yet forced me into a deep dive into my feelings. After a month of being in darkness again, thinking of how good it would feel when it is over, my partner told me, "every day you find more and more pain, and it does not seem like it is helping you". Gratefull for the love and connection we have, I heard him and turned around the plate.

YOU WERE ALWAYS ENOUGH

I was now a mom of two boys, and decided to be the best version of myself every day. I saw the illusion of happiness in the future and the resistance I had to the nature of life. I started to see how important it is to accept every aspect of life, to let yourself be free. What it means to feel the energy of love instead of fear. How to stand solid in your centre even if the world is falling apart.

We believe in the lie that we are somehow not worthy, loved and safe, because we mess up, while in fact all those feelings just covered the true essence of who we are.

There is nothing wrong with us, we are beautiful in our individual human design.

I know now, it was not my choice but an automated response. I still have this arrise, but I can accept it is human to do so. With training I came to a state, where I could create out of it, to be more present, aware and even meditate properly. Uncovering long-forgotten happy memories from the past, energy to live and be present.

I understood how important it is to keep your focus straight and to feel the energy of love. Love contains every aspect of duality in this world and it helps us realise our true nature and the nature of life.

I became aware of my power and energy, as well as how to manage it. I learnt that fear is nothing more than an emotion to keep us safe. Whatever happened in life, my soul knew the truth deep inside.

Every experience was important to make me the woman I am today.

Speaking my truth was always the right thing to do, even if some people are not ready to hear it.

We all have our own timeline.

BRANKA PESTAR HAJŠEK

Branka is on a mission to transform the way we see emotions and human potential to reveal the true power of humanity.

Her knowledge combines the natural laws of life, corporate science, and personal experiences.

Endometriosis changed her life dramatically and she saw life and herself in a new light. It started her emotional empowerment journey.

Branka believes in compassion, inner power, and unlimited potential. She offers, personal consultations, leadership training, and workshops.

Her job is not to fix you or tell you what to do, her role is to give you space, provide you with understanding, while you explore your unique self and inner power.

Between many roles, she is a partner to a wonderful man, mom of two boys and businesswoman. Her business supports her in a way to be present as a mom, taking care of her body, and sharing the message to which she feels deeply connected.

LinkedIn: www.linkedin.com/in/brankapestar?originalSubdomain=si
Facebook: www.facebook.com/branka.pestar

13

STACEY PIEDRAHITA

REIKI IS BETTER THAN SEX

"Owning our story and loving ourselves through the process is the bravest thing we'll ever do" Brene Brown

---

J am sixteen floors above the Atlantic Ocean on the balcony dancing like I'm Meryl Streep in Mamma Mia. A familiar feeling I have come to know and love washes over me; it's pure bliss. I was finally free from all the years of self-sabotaging, free from the chains that have held me hostage the majority of my life. I started sobbing and dropped to my knees. I have witnessed a miracle. I have done what some say is impossible. I have rewritten the narrative. I have connected to the divine source and have claimed the multidimensional life that we were born to lead. I rewired my brain to make me a happier person. This is inner peace, I have become the hero of my own story. It is now time to own it.

I spent my life running away from God. I have suffered from clinical depression and PTSD silently since I was a child. I had been living life just going through the motions, in a constant state of stress and survival mode. How can someone believe in a higher power when they have lived a lifetime of suffering? No one knew about the demons that were terrorizing me on the inside. I was too ashamed to talk to anyone. I learned to manage and hide the pain. I did a great job of numbing it. I spent the majority of my life hiding behind a mask of shame, blame, and never feeling good enough, I built walls around my heart and if people got too close, I shut them out. It was the path I chose. The path I chose was just about to catch up to me.

In 2018, I was admitted to the hospital and spent five days in a drug-induced state. The pain was awful. My belly was so distended I looked 9 months pregnant. I was discharged with instructions to go see a therapist because they said it could be stress and anxiety. For sixteen years doctors were just prescribing me pills without truly knowing what was wrong. I accepted that this was my life. After discharge I declined rapidly and my body shut down. The cognitive impairment was the worst. I still suffer from the lingering effects to this day. I felt hopeless and powerless. I just didn't want to be here anymore. I was at one of the lowest points in my life. I had dealt with suicidal attempts from both my mother and son. Life had been really hard, but the thought of taking my own life was reprehensible to me. It ripped my heart out to feel this way, I was so broken. The guilt I felt for wanting to leave my children, husband and life were overwhelming. One day my husband walked into the bedroom and asked, "Why don't you try being more positive?" If my bedridden ass was strong enough I would have thrown his ass out the window.

I called my sister and cried and told her I just wanted God to take me. So I did what she told me and picked a gospel song that resonated with me I listened to it over and over. Miraculously after about an hour I started to feel something stirring in me. It was a very unfamiliar feeling, unconditional love and peace are how I would describe it. My stomach immediately decreased in size. If my husband didn't witness this, I would have thought it was just my imagination. I just witnessed a miracle. Is this what the presence of God feels like? I fell asleep for the first time in my life with a little bit of faith. I had heard people speak about the presence of God but never believed it. I wanted more! I stopped listening to the doctors and took matters into my own hands. I had enough knowledge from nursing to know that if I wanted to heal I had to fix myself first. I started reading self-healing books I started doing gratitude and affirmation lists daily, and I made a conscious effort to laugh every day. Inside I was dying and full of sadness. I truly should have been an actress. I incorporated an Autoimmmune Protocol diet. I slowly started to recover. Gratitude and laughter were the most elements instrumental to my recovery. The next few months were spent recovering. This is when my spiritual journey started.

One morning I woke up and drove to the nearest church. I was ready. I wanted the unwavering faith I had heard others talk about. For so many years I tried to do the right thing for my kids and learn about religion. I knew I had to give it another try this time so I gave it all I had. I immersed myself in the gospel. I bought a bible and joined a bible study. I went to church every weekend. I was doing everything right yet something was still missing. Why was I walking into the church but walking out feeling more judged than ever? The only thing I enjoyed was the music. The music made my heart sing. I was raised Jewish so Christianity was foreign to me. I even converted and was baptized with my children. I thought I was doing the right thing. I was waiting for that instant TADA feeling of being saved. It never happened. I just didn't feel like I belonged. Isn't God supposed to love everybody? I know I am a hot mess but I knew in my heart I was a good person. For about a year and a half, I committed to learning about Christianity. It turned into more of a burden than a blessing. If I have learned one thing from this, I can say with the utmost certainty that when you are ready, everything will fall into place.

"When the student is ready the teacher will appear. When the student is truly ready... the teacher will disappear" Lao Tzu

---

Fast forward to 2021, It was the end of March. The weekend prior I went on a four mile hike and was feeling great! After, I ended up in the hospital, but I was prepared this time. Remember this isn't my first rodeo. Instead of my normal, "Are you fucking kidding me?" I chose a different reaction I thought, "What are you trying to teach me?" After eight days in the hospital after getting tired of having more pills thrown at me, I took matters into my own hands. I was determined to heal myself. I had all the tools. I was done with conventional medicine. I was going to try the alternative. I went to see a functional medicine doctor who informed me I was being poisoned... The toxic medications I had been put on a few months prior were doing this, plus my breast implants were shutting my body down. I finally got an answer, but not the one I was expecting. I was in a critical condition. I had to get my implants out ASAP. I had Breast Implant Illness.

I had gone to see a Reiki Practioner earlier that year and had felt an immediate shift in my vibration. It instantly helped with my stress and anxiety. I hadn't taken any anxiety, pain or depressions pill since 2018. Reiki aligned perfectly with my holistic healing path. My Reiki Master, Cathy, is a miracle worker. She came to my house to do Reiki! What a beautiful soul! I discovered Dr. Joe Dispenza, Gabby Bernstein and Noor Hibbert. I became an expert in Quantum Physics and Neuroplasticity. I started visualizing myself as healthy. "I am whole, and healthy" became my new mantra. I also masturbated. I was in bed all the time. What else was I supposed to do? I couldn't have sex because I would've had a fucking heart attack! I needed some form of exercise. Anything to release that dopamine and oxytocin! Don't judge me y'all, it's medicinal! I really couldn't do anything except expand my knowledge while I was stuck in bed. Physically, my health was getting worse but mentally I was getting stronger. I was at the point of requiring 24/7 care. I knew I was running out of time and then something miraculous happened. I started to hear little voices in my head. At first, I thought I was going crazy. I started to really pay attention to them and realized this was my intuition! I also discovered Transcendental Meditation. I was becoming a pro at this guru stuff! One day, I asked for the name of my spirit guides and I got Ralph and Rachel. I didn't understand the correlation until a few weeks later. I started researching Numerology and Angels. I discovered Delta 8! I learned more about myself in 3 months than my entire lifetime. I definitely stepped out of my comfort zone. I started asking the Universe for deliberate signs. I was having so much fun with this. I was laughing more. I'm talking belly laughs. I started learning more about my Chakras and Energy Healing while desperately trying to find a surgeon who could do my explant ASAP, I threw it out into the Universe. I was going to be healed! I will have my explant soon! I pictured myself sharing my story and spreading awareness. Talk about a surreal moment writing this and realizing I made this happen! I rarely paid my symptoms any attention. I started believing what I was writing down. I was the happiest, bedridden person I knew. Then rock bottom hit.

There was a part of me that didn't believe I was going to make it through the night. I told my daughter I was declining fast. The blood-curdling screams that I heard from her will haunt me for the rest of my life. That was my lowest point. At that moment I surrendered. This time I was begging to live! I fell asleep praying that God would give me more time. Around 3 am I woke up. I saw the brightest light you can imagine. My life flashed in front of me. Every pivotal moment, the trauma and tragedies. I remembered everything but I had instant peace. A weight had been lifted. I can't really explain it. Instant enlightenment, maybe? Everything that had ever happened to me in my life suddenly made sense. Like a puzzle, everything had fallen into place. I apologized to God for not going to church and finding Jesus. I knew, without a shadow of a doubt, that I had been forgiven and I instantly forgave myself. This God would never cause the suffering I blamed him for all of my life. This was unconditional love. This is what had been missing my whole life. God lives in me, I was told. I finally met Ralph, my fairy Godfather. It turns out that in my head, Ralph is Dr. Wayne Dyer. His wisdom and guidance were instrumental in my recovery. This must be the unwavering faith I had been searching for all of my life. I knew God was going to heal me. I found out three days later my surgery was booked for May 7th. Every day after that has been full of wonderment and joy. I woke up from my surgery, took my first breath and opened my eyes for the very first time. I found my "why" and I knew nothing would ever be the same again. I had just witnessed another miracle.

A few weeks later, during my Reiki attunement ceremony, we were in the middle of our meditation. I was walking towards a mountain in a beautiful field of wildflowers. I saw a girl surrounded by beautiful radiant light running towards me. I realized all of a sudden it was me!! I started crying. She grabbed my hand and walked me up the mountain. After the ceremony, I asked Cathy, my Reiki Master. What the hell just happened? She said I'd just met my inner child. Words can't describe the emotions I was feeling. I found out a few weeks prior that my Hebrew name is Shimon. I have set her free and she now lives in me permanently. I don't even recognize the old me. I let the tears flow like Niagara Falls now. If I am having a bad day, I own it and realize tomorrow will be better. I live my life full of divine intervention and guidance. I have come to the realization it is okay to not be okay. It is okay to fall apart, and there is healing in those tears. All my life I had to be strong because I thought vulnerability was a weakness. It turned out to be my biggest strength.

My journey to self-love and finding God has been anything but easy. It has taken a while to process what has happened, but if it wasn't for my near-death experience I never would have released my inner child and found unwavering faith. For that, I am forever grateful. Knowing God's love and the love I now have for myself, is what ultimately set me free. It just took one foot at death's door to truly start living my best life. Every day moving forward is a gift.

Trauma was the root cause of most of my issues. The rest were the choices I have made throughout my lifetime. I am taking full accountability and owning my shit. The breast implants made depression and anxiety unbearable. I know in my heart I never would have been as bad as I was if I didn't get them. Again, another bad choice. I encourage all women to learn the symptoms of BII. It might just save your life, or that of someone you love. Be your own advocate and do your research when it comes to prescription medications. The toxic medications for my misdiagnosed Autoimmune Disease, along with chronic stress were responsible for my body shutting down. I am happy to say I am off all prescription medications. I have taken the more holistic path. I'm getting lost in God's country to nourish my soul. I chose not to address my mental health issues and I paid the price with almost losing my life twice now. My body is my temple and I will never take it for granted ever again. Please learn from my mistakes. I have rewritten my story and I am making it the best one imaginable. Three years ago, I knew I had a story to tell but everything happened in Divine timing. I'm surrounded by love and light everywhere I go. I am guided all day long. On those really stressful days, I close my eyes, go to my quiet place and instantly the 'Knowing" feeling washes over me and I know that everything will be alright. I trust in the power of my story. I'm sharing my heart and vulnerability with others in hopes of empowering and inspiring them to let go of the past and learn to fall in love with the most authentic version of you. There is healing in the story of your scars. Release that inner child and start living, instead of just being alive! Get your sparkle back. There is always light at the end of the tunnel. This I can promise you. Even if you have to light that bitch up yourself! I trust in the power of my inner wisdom now, and my positive intentions have the power to bring some light into a very dark world.

God loves me just the way I am. The flawed me. The one with the battle scars. It just took getting to the end, or so I thought, to fall in love with me. I'm living proof God loves hot messes!

STACEY PIEDRAHITA

Stacey has been a healer for 26 years as an RN but recently found her true calling as a Reiki Practitioner and Spiritual Teacher after surviving a debilitating illness and near-death experience.

Her darkest hours have been her greatest teachers. She is embarking on a new Enlightened path teaching people how to release their inner child, their limiting beliefs and learn how to FLY, (Fucking Loving Yourself) first.

Stacey knows everyone has a purpose and wants to awaken souls to promote a kinder world for humanity. Join Stacey on a journey of healing through her signature Reiki "Lovegasms" and unique healing methods in The Manifesting Virgin Academy. She is living her best life after finding more joy and happiness than she ever imagined possible. Stacey is dedicated to healing others and lifting the stigma on mental health.

She is living proof God loves everyone, most of all, Hot messes!

Website: www.themanifestingvirgin.com
Instagram: www.instagram.com/themanifestingvirgin

14

VINNIE MAHLER

LOVE YOURSELF, THE VOICE SAID

"*L*ove Yourself, the voice said.

I was sitting in the dark in my bed crying my eyes out when I heard a crystal-clear voice saying. "Love Yourself". I froze! Slowly I moved my head from side to side to check the room. 'Who on Earth was in my flat?' I was 100% sure that I was all on my own, so who had just spoken? I felt goosebumps all over and I looked down at the picture I had been holding in my hands. 'You, it was You who spoke.' I instantly knew it and I felt the picture smiling back at me...

Earlier that year I had been on a transformational retreat. During the retreat, I had been introduced to a little book called *Heaven is for Real*, and on the last page of the book was a picture of Jesus. That picture had been with me since and had supported me through some of the pretty tough times of my life to date.

The voice came at the darkest time of my life. It came as I had failed my last attempt to fulfil my plan to finish myself off. Finish my suffering, finish the pain, finish the constant fight for love – no one loves me anyway, no one care for me anyway, no one will even notice that I'm not here anymore, so what's the point to keep fighting, what's the point about living my life. I wanted sooooo much to get away. It was so intense, that at times I was screaming, "I WANT TO GET AWAY, I just want to get away, allow me to get away", whereafter I would curl up on the floor crying as I couldn't stand the pain anymore... Most of all I wanted to get away from HIM!

The alcoholic, the addict, the abuser, the user, the narcissist—I was just the servant, I was just the body that had to give sex on demand, I was the housekeeper, I had to be invisible till I was needed. I did not matter at all, I was No One, I had no value at all as a person. I was stripped of all dignity and left with no self-esteem.

So, standing on the bridge and looking down, looking down in contemplation on the rock... "What rock will be the best to finish me off the quickest when I hit my head on it?" I sense a person walking along the edge of the water in my inner eye, even before I managed to finish my chain of planning thoughts. I held my breath and my head sank deeper than ever before as I realised, "I can't give the person that will find me the shock, pain and trauma it will be to find my body. I can't! I have to find a way to live. I have to live. I have no choice but to live! But how, how can I live, how can I live this life, how how HOWWW??"

THE JOURNEY OF LIFE

The voice of Jesus came with the answer to my question; "Love Yourself". The answer did not make sense for me at that moment, because "Who am I and what on Earth is love?" I had no clue who I was, and even less did I know what love was. I had grown up so co-dependent that I always tuned in to what other people wanted from me and what they wanted me to do. I was so fearful of their reactions that I was willing to do anything to please them. I was also so desperate to be loved that I never gave myself a thought as I was constantly pleasing others and gave them what I thought they wanted. Please note that I write *thought* they wanted, as I never asked anyone, I always presumed but never received confirmation from them to show if I was right or wrong. The lack of confirmation made me even more desperate and made me make an even bigger effort to please them. I would do anything to be acknowledged, liked and loved.

Love, what is love? As a child my mum and teachers always told me when I came crying because I had been bullied "It's just because they love you and don't know how to show it". What I didn't tell my teachers and mum was that I actually got beaten up. This and the abuse I experienced lead to me believing at a very early age, that love is equal to being blue and green all over. At some level I knew it was wrong, as I never showed my bruises to my parents. I did all I could to hide them. I was seeking situations where I would get beaten up and abused. If I wasn't beaten up, I wasn't loved, right?

My strong feeling of wanting to get away plus the voice speaking to me made me DESPERATE to 'get fixed'. I was willing to pay anything to get fixed, because I felt soooo broken. A mentor of mine reinforced this. She told me that she didn't realise how sick I was in my mind, but now that she knew, we had to get a hammer and chisel to work through the layers. That night I cried and cried and cried, as I felt so f#*%'ed up. "Why me?"

I started to believe that I was born to be a servant, I glued myself to her as I thought she was able to fix me and I did EVERYTHING she told me to do. I was fearful of her not wanting to speak with me ever again. I was fearful as I believed she was the only one that could help me. I was so fearful, that once again I was pleasing others and purely listening to them to find myself. I believed all she told me about me...

I still wanted to get AWAY from him, the alcoholic, addict and abuser and I had at this point isolated myself with him. I was so full of shame of not being able to leave him, and his behaviour that I had cut myself off from EVERYONE around me, except from work, him, my mentor and self help group. I felt so disgusted with myself, as I could see what was going on, and even then I still felt paralysed to take action. I was blaming him for my miserable life, I was blaming him for all my pain, I was blaming his drug addiction and the alcohol for his abusive behaviour, so I did not have to take responsibility for my own life.

Every night before I went to bed, I was down on my knees praying. I prayed for a way out of this relationship, I prayed for a solution, I prayed as the tears was running down my cheeks that something would happen, I prayed that I would be strong enough to end the relationship.

My prayers were answered.

Ever since I was a little girl, my biggest dream has been to become a mother. In all my relationships I have many times secretly hoped that I would fall pregnant. Thinking of holding my own little baby girl in my arms always seem to bring a smile on my face. Knowing that I created a life within me, the thought of the experience of bringing a new life to Earth is indescribable for me. It brings me so much joy imagining the feeling of her in my arms, even she isn't here yet...

My partner and I went to visit his family. We had rented a hotel room for the weekend to have our own space away from his family. It was Friday night and we were in bed and had sex. I suddenly had this clear feeling and I instantly knew what just happened... I totally freaked out – in silence, on the inside – I AM PREGNANT! But I don't want him to become a dad again. I had seen enough of how he was with his current daughter and NO WAY in the world did I want him to ruin another child too. This is not going to happen, not with me!

The next day I went to the chemist and got a regret pill. I was absolutely panicking and so determined not to have a child with him. It so happened that the pill made me SO sick and I vomited all that night, which made me panic even more... I knew I had vomited the pill up! I went to the chemist again and I got another pill that should work up to 5 days after conception. However, she was not going to leave that easily! I was now out of myself.

What can I do, what do I do? This is my biggest dream to be pregnant and become a mother. Yet no way in a million years am I going to allow HIM become a dad again, NEVER EVER!

- Do I end the relationship, have the child, not tell him and keep the child?
- Do I end the relationship, have the child, not tell him and give it away?
- Do I end the relationship, have the child and tell him? NO WAY, then he will be a dad.
- Do I end the relationship, have an abortion and not tell him?
- Do I end the relationship, have an abortion and tell him?

I could not even consider to stay in the relationship! No way!

The pain was real, the pain in my heart, the pain in my whole being, the pain of having to make a decision, a decision that I did not want to make. How would I be able to live with myself no matter what I choose, how??

I gave myself 24 hours to make the decision. No reason to take longer, as it would not benefit to drag the pain out longer than necessary by walking around indecisive.

The tears were running like a waterfall, over my face that day. I was sitting in my chair while looking out the window, not eating, not drinking, nothing else other than sitting in that chair and allowing all the different options to run through my head. I then wrote all the options down and stared at them. The feeling of peace grew and I knew what to do. Not that it was a decision that I actually wanted, but it was the decision that I had the most peace with. I had to end the relationship for sure, how can I be in a relationship with a man I could not even allow to be a dad for my children. That was suddenly crystal clear for me, I had to end it, there was no other options. I also had to get an abortion, and I had peace with the decision. I had peace with it because I had felt a higher power promise me that one other day, I would become a mother. Now was not the right time, this pregnancy was for me to have the strength to get out of this toxic relationship. She was a gift from heaven in so many ways and she was not meant to live in a body yet. She came to support me through this time. I write *she* as I had a strong feeling that it was a girl. I connected with her and spoke with her till I had to send her back.

I believe that she stayed till I had fully finished the chapter with that man. The man that I knew from day one I did not want to be in a relationship with, but because I didn't feel I had a choice I had to. I was never the one who could choose, it was always chosen for me. I had to accept what was given to me and take whoever wanted me. Four years learning, four years of growth, four years of finally understanding that I get to live every single day, instead of just existing, four years to finally appreciate that I matter and that I get to choose who I want to be around.

Never had I thought possible that I would turn my life around so I would choose to live. Never had I thought it possible that I would experience what true love is. Never had I thought that I would be able to have a life of my own—because who was I?

I am free, I am finally free, I am free to live!

Before this point in my journey, I had been focusing on how to die, and then how to get out of the really toxic, negative relationship. Suddenly I was free to focus on finding myself and what I wanted. I got to dive deep into who I am and what I like.

Not only was I free to live, but I also had started a journey in discovering myself and my previously unknown natural gifts. I had not thought about all that happened as a child when I was fearful of the dark, because I could feel beings in the dark that no one could see–I called them monsters. Today I know differently and I am embracing my gifts more and more in excitement of all the people I am helping with my gifts. I thought I was crazy and different, I thought I was the only one, I thought I was special – yet, I am one of many that are open to learn more and more of what we truly are capable of when we deeply know ourselves and are open to Love and loving ourselves.

LESSONS LEARNT...

Don't trust people and the words they say—Ask questions and feel if there is truth in the answers received. It is possible to feel this in our body after some practice. We all know how it feels like when we enter a room where there has been a fight, Think back now to how you felt after being around a big fight. We also know how it feels like looking at a sunset/sunrise, or cuddling a child or a pet, do you feel it now? This is our first guide to know what feels good and what feels not so good. Now you get to ask questions and feel the answer in your body.

The hardest lesson for me was to realise that I will never die. It is only my body that dies. The pain, the learnings and the stories will stay until I have released them. So even if I took my own life, I would keep going in the same cycle of stories, pain and struggles till I deal with them. I cried massively when I realised this.

The best lesson I have learnt is that I am the creator of everything I experience. I create my life with my thoughts, feelings, and vibration. I get to choose how I act on what happens in my life. I get to choose what feelings and emotions I allow myself to experience. In the beginning this was gibberish and did not make sense at all, however as I play with it, I get more and more excited as I actually get to choose how I want my life to be. It just takes some practice and then I become better and better.

I am proud of...

How far I have come in my journey in life. I know that I have caused a lot of pain in my family and friends, because I simply did not know how to behave. I did what I felt I had to do at any given time. I also know that I had to go through this journey, so I could learn to know myself without anyone telling me who they wanted me to be and what they wanted me to do.

I am also proud that I have managed to move to Australia and be in places that have supported my growth and happiness while I create the life I want to live. Australia had been a part of my childhood as I was always looking at pictures from when my dad was living here. We children felt special when we got to hold the Emu egg, he had brought home and we were wearing his hat. I have always had a feeling of being home here. I have learnt on my journey that home is wherever I am, as home is inside of me. But even so, I have been longing for a place that I could call home that I feel is a home. I lived in my flat in Copenhagen for 17 years and never felt home...

Australia has a special vibe I am attracted to. I love spending time in remote areas, in national parks where the only sound I can hear is nature. I connect with Mother Earth in a whole different way than I have done in other places. I connect with the people and the story of Australia easily, and I really have sympathy for the original people of the land I walk on here. The way they lived their life and how they still are living, fascinates me. I feel blessed to have met so many amazing people here, who have been able to teach me more than I could ever imagine.

Now that I feel that I'm home, I agree with the saying that there is nowhere like home. Home as it is inside me and home in this country of Australia where I choose to be.

VINNIE MAHLER

Meet Vinnie, You may or may not know her in this life, yet. As you are reading these words though, you will become aware that you would have come across each other in a previous life.

Vinnie had NO clue who she was, and one day a voice out of the blue asked her, 'Love Yourself'. Since then, she has learnt that EVERYTHING is energy, frequency and vibration. We can change our life, by directing our energy towards what we want. Now she is an Intuitive Light Facilitator, Online Entrepreneur as a Water Snob and Norm Breaker as well as a catalyst for SelfLove, Choice, and to smile to Feel good. She holds space for many women who choose to make change in their lives to have more SelfLove and to Feel better.

Connect with Vinnie:
Facebook:
www.facebook.com/WorldVinnie/
www.facebook.com/vinnie.live.love.laugh.light

Vinnie wants to say "Thank you for being You, because there is only you to BE You! You are Loved, You are respected and You are supported JUST BECAUSE YOU ARE YOU!"

15

SHANI TAYLOR

NO ONE CARES ABOUT YOU

*U*nless you can tell them why they should, in the context of what is most meaningful to them, and what is most meaningful to them is themselves. Yet, every time you go to speak, in any context, whether it be with your partner or children, at work with your clients or colleagues, or at the gym to your fitness friends, you keep sharing what you have to say in the context of you. It then falls on deaf ears and you wonder why you aren't feeling deeply connected to yourself or others to the degree that you would love to.

As a human being, you are hard-wired to automatically and constantly be thinking about yourself; speaking for and about yourself, and seeking to get connection. You communicate what you want and need with very little consideration for the other individuals you are speaking to. This is the nature of being human, and we are all the same. You are speaking AT people rather than WITH them – and they are doing the same to you.

From the moment you are born and throughout your entire childhood, you are not taught how to truly connect with other individuals. As a baby, you are taught that the world is about you. You cry, wink, gurgle or make any movement and you are pampered with attention. You learn that the world revolves around you. As you move through your toddler years to pre-teens you are experiencing life through your feelings and relating to others and the world through the lens of how it all impacts you, with very little thought beyond yourself to consider how others are experiencing life.

You then go into adolescence. By this stage, life has become increasingly challenging as you navigate hormones surging within you and the emotions they create, whilst simultaneously attempting to understand the external world and trying to find your place in society as adulthood knocks on your door.

By default, your mind is constantly thinking about you, what you want, what you need and your desires. In fact, when you aren't focused on solving a definitive problem, ninety-five percent of the time you are thinking about YOURSELF. As is every other individual on this earth.

So now, every single day, we have close to eight billion people roaming this world speaking AT one another rather than WITH each other.

What does that even mean?

At its most simplistic form, it means that every individual is thinking and speaking about what they value rather than identifying what the other person values and then communicating their values in the context of their intended audience.

If you learned the art form of identifying the values of others and how to communicate your needs in their values, and if you applied it daily, then you would be able to connect with others quickly and with ease. You would make more profound connections with a wide range of individuals. If you applied this within your intimate relationship and family you would feel a greater sense of fulfilment and equally feel seen and heard by your loved ones. In the context of your business, you would have an abundance of people to serve - consistently.

The key is in knowing what your values are. When you know how to determine what is most meaningful to you, it becomes easier to understand what others value.

You have a mission in this life. Every single individual does. It might be dedication to raising your family, helping people in their health and wellbeing, dissolving wounds from their past, or you might work in an organisation as an intrapreneur making your mark on the world by working within a wider collective purpose.

Whatever your mission is, you'll have a greater impact if you learn how to share your message in a way that's meaningful not only to you but to the individuals you want to share your mission with. You then have a meeting of the hearts and minds and each individual within the connection feels a greater sense of fulfilment.

THE UNIVERSE SPEAKS

At the age of 11, I was given one of the greatest gifts anyone could ever receive however at the time, my pre-teen mind didn't truly grasp the magnificence of what I had been given.

That gift was the 1920s classic book written by Dale Carnegie, *How to Win Friends and Influence People*. The title repelled me at the time, I didn't want to 'win' friends, I wanted people to like me for me, without competition. And I certainly didn't see any value in trying to influence others because that term made me feel like I was being deceitful. However, I decided to read the book anyway and I'm glad I did.

How to Win Friends and Influence People has stood the test of time because it isn't about being in competition with others to gain their approval, nor is it about being deceitful.

The entire contents of the book are underpinned by human behaviour principles and how to best use them to make genuine and heartfelt connections with other human beings. In doing so, both you and the other person get what you want. That's a win-win in any relationship.

In the context of today's digital world, mastering the art of human connection isn't optional, it's a must.

Every single day there are around sixty billion messages sent out across digital platforms. People are bombarded with messages all day long. Every time you look at your smartphone you'll see an array of notifications from the various apps you have. If you open up your social media profiles, you are immediately screamed at with content by others who have created that with themselves in mind, rather than creating it in a way that speaks with you. Think about this, when you're on social media scrolling, how many times do you actually stop and consume someone else's content in your newsfeed for more than two seconds? A handful of times, correct?

When it comes to your business and wanting to capture and keep the attention of your target audience, you can now start to grasp the difficulty you have in achieving this monstrous feat. It's not as simple as just putting up some content that you created and hoping for the best.

Remember, you have been programmed to speak AT people rather than WITH them so your audience isn't naturally stopping just because you shared something. They are too busy thinking about themselves.

Your audience is busy, tired from their own responsibilities and fatigued from the noise coming at them online.

This is one of the key reasons that most service providers and business owners fail within their first few years of business or why it stays as their side hustle and never fully reaches it potential.

The problem for many healers, coaches, consultants and entrepreneurs is they love providing their service and they know they are great at it, but they often don't know how to become visible to the right audience or how to share their message in a way that connects. You struggle to know where to find the people who are looking for what it is you have to offer and how to create a strong online presence so you end up having inconsistent months in terms of billing and growing your business and your impact.

Often you keep searching for answers in the wrong places – you keep getting taught more tactics. Tactics are part of the problem, not part of the solution. Tactics change and are responsive to external circumstances like the online platform, algorithm, and the economy. Yes, staying up to date with tactics is required, however, there is a key element missing from most business growth teachings. That is intuitive principles.

Principles are universal and don't change. When you combine the required tactic but underpin it with universal laws and human behaviour principles then you immediately make an authentic connection with the people you'd love to serve.

When you do this, you are truly seen and heard by your audience and share your message and mission in a way that connects.

This is why that book I was given at the age of 11, was one of the greatest gifts I have ever received. In my work today, I mentor clients on how to truly connect with their target audience by combining both intuitive principles and tangible strategy. The beautiful thing is, they often share that this work for their business has not only helped them create consistency and growth but they use these same principles in their personal life and it deepens their connection to their partner and children.

That is the power of mastering the art of human connection.

SOMETHING'S MISSING

You don't know who you are.

You have constant up and downs and feel something is missing and then you attempt to run away from that feeling of not enough, of missing something, and you label it as bad.

You keep running from your missing-ness because you're blind to seeing how it is actually serving you. Your quest in this life, whether it be in raising your family, career, or something else you love doing, is an expression of your spiritual mission and your spiritual mission is directly correlated to your highest value. Your highest value is not a social idealism like 'good person, kind, caring, loves family'. If you think it is it is because you've likely injected the expectation of an external opinion into your life and that's partly why your own vision can be clouded, because you're trying to live up to the expectations of the external world rather than knowing your true voids and values and living your life around these.

Your highest value is what you perceive to be most missing in your life. That's why you value it, because you think you don't have enough of it.

This concept exists in economics, philosophy and human behaviour.

Your deepest void won't have changed over the course of your life. It was formed in your early years based on your experiences and how you perceived them. Your void is a feeling or perception, not a tangible action.

You won't value something unless you perceive there is a void in it. If you perceive you have enough of something then there is no need for you to value it because in your perception you have enough of it. You value what you value because it is your void. It is this void that has driven you to create your mission and message for this world. It is serving you. It gives you your purpose. Without it, you would cease to exist and no organism will self-annihilate so you are on a lifelong quest to fill it. You are on a mission to fill up that void with your value. But when you perceive you are almost full you will create scenarios and experiences in your life to give you that sense of emptiness again, that missing-ness, so that you maintain your purpose and drive to keep filling your mission or purpose.

Think of it like this. You have a water bottle and inside is the water. The water represents your void-value-value. You keep filling up your water bottle with water but you will never let it get full. In those moments where you perceive it to be almost full, you will empty almost all your water - your void-value - out so you can start again and keep going. The water is the thing you perceive to be most missing and the tangible water bottle is the vehicle for the expression of your spiritual mission. If you look over the course of your life you will see that the tangible vehicle has changed shape and form but what you've been filling the bottle up with has remained the same. Throughout your life, it has been a plastic water bottle, a two-litre spring water bottle, a plastic cup. But the water that you keep putting in has been the same.

What does this even mean? I'll give you an example.

My deepest void is connection and I didn't really learn this at the conscious level until just a few years ago. My subconscious knew it and had been driving me my whole life but I wasn't aware of it or consciously in control of it. So, throughout my entire life, I have been on a mission to fill my perceived void of connection. When I look at the different vehicles I have chosen for the expression of this over the course of my life, there have been many. Friendships as a teenager, boyfriends, jobs in sales positions, learning at university as a mature-age student, I even had a drug addiction at one point which was used to fill the void of connection. Other vehicles for the expression and fulfilment of connection have been my son, yoga and then becoming a yoga teacher, and today the expression for my spiritual mission is my business.

With this newfound understanding, I encourage you to ask yourself "What do I perceive has been most missing in my life?". Listen to your inner wisdom, it knows the truth.

YOUR GIFT TO THE WORLD

The greatest gift you can give this world is you.

That's right. YOU.

When you are serving and problem-solving in the area you love applying yourself in, whether it's your family, career or something else, you feel a tingling inside. Your mind and body light up. The thing is, you can't seem to get enough of this. You want and need more people with which to share your gift. To share your message and mission with the world on a greater scale.

So, what's getting in your way of achieving this?

Hard truth. It's YOU.

How do I know? Because I also get in my own way.

From time to time life feels incredibly challenging. At times, when I am confronted with highly stressful situations I can feel that there's no light at the end of the tunnel. Darkness fills my mind. Sometimes I can allow personal challenges to infiltrate me showing up in my business and those challenges get in the way of me fulfilling my spiritual quest.

Those challenges I experience can sometimes be a slow 'burn' and creep up on me until one day it smacks me in the face and I realise I have to dissolve them quickly or I will have gone so far backward that the crawl back to balance will be a feat within itself.

The beauty of challenges is we get given profound learnings if we choose to intuitively listen to them.

Fast forward through all the trials and errors and here's what I learned and what you can benefit from.

The very problem you help people solve will also be the very problem that gets in your way of serving them and in you growing your mission. My entire business is built on connection and showing others how to connect. If I'm not connecting with myself or others, then my business isn't growing.

During personal challenges, I can feel drained and disconnected from myself. When I feel disconnected from myself I perceive that the resource of connection is finite and scarce. I perceive that the resource of connection is not easily within my grasp and then I pull back from trying to connect with others so that I can keep what I have left for myself.

Herein-lay your problem.

Your service offering or mission is not at random. Your service offering or mission is centred around your highest value. And your highest value is a reflection of your deepest void. What you perceive to be most missing in your life.

That's why you value it. This is why you are intrinsically inspired from within to serve in your space. You value things that you perceive you don't have 'enough' of. If you felt there was an abundance of the 'thing' then you wouldn't be on a quest to consume it because you'd perceive you don't need it because you'd have enough of it.

In the context of your business or career, your mission is directly correlated to what you perceive to be most missing in your life.

Because of this, at times, you will be in scarcity mode and therefore what little you have left you'll want to protect and keep, rather than give to others. Here is the truth: nothing is actually missing and your void and value are infinite.

You need the perceptions of missing-ness and fullness in order to share your gift with this world and create the impact you were born to have.

Wisdom is being able to recognise this and communicate it in a way that is authentic for you but meaningful to your intended audience, whether that's your family, colleagues, clients or anyone else.

The best way for you to do this is to first know what your deepest void and value is, and then be able to express this to your intended audience - because they are having the same experience as you.

That's why they want your service. That's why you're inspired to serve them. As Rumi said, "what you seek is seeking you."

To not master this is to let both yourself and your target audience down. You're missing out on connecting with them and they're missing out on having their problem solved. This is true whether it's your children, your clients, or your gym floor friends. If you only communicate from your I-centric place and continue to speak at people rather than with them, no matter how powerful your message it is, it will continue to fall on deaf ears. Speaking your truth is important, but so too is having others listen to it.

When you can master your message and communicate in a way that is both authentic to you and meaningful to them, then you have an abundance of people to serve, deeper connections and greater impact in this world. This is what it means to meaningfully speak your truth.

So, now I ask you, are you ready to master your message and have a greater impact in this world?

SHANI TAYLOR

Healers, Therapists, Coaches, Consultants and Entrepreneurs come to Shani to help them connect with an ever-greater number of people in their market, and to increase their business growth with compelling client connection and attraction strategies. Helping others to powerfully connect and communicate their message and mission with the world is what she does best.

Working together, you'll have a newfound and deep understanding of your market and what they truly want, get exact clarity on how to communicate powerfully to them and how to create content that connects and converts. You'll learn how to combine business and client attraction strategies with human behaviour and universal principles which make you stand out in any setting, and draws your perfect fit clients to you.

When Shani isn't being of service, you can find her reading, researching topics such as human behaviour or mind-body health, and ; or practising yoga.

Want to connect with Shani? Find her on Facebook and send her a message, she is ready to chat with you:
www.facebook.com/shani.taylor.opentograce

16

KALI J WALTERS

BIRTHING TO REBIRTH EMPOWERED VOICES

*a*s I lie in my bed to write this, I'm listening to my babies outside and recalling how it felt to go from reliant on the mainstream to standing up and saying No, I have to do this my way!

I'd always been the rebel, the one to do things differently. I was always the one that took great pride in standing up against authority and saying a big F U to those who tried to control me.

Ironically I had also always been the biggest rebel against myself, not allowing myself to truly stand up and speak. Not allowing my own voice and knowing to shine through, you could say I was the freest caged person you could find. The one that everyone would have said, you can't tell her what to do and yet would say ask her, she'll do it for you.

So this is my story of returning to my sovereign state, before the world plunged to its epic craziness that it's in as I write these words. Before I claimed to be a Freedomprenuer. Before I truly saw what freedom and sovereignty could look like. This happened to show me I could speak my truth, guided by my inner knowing and I would be okay...

This is the story of me rebirthing my freedom, and taking my power back...

Take it back to 2018, I had three beautiful children, and was pregnant with what I'd then say was my last child. My last girl, which I always knew to be a girl even though I never found out the gender.

I knew before any test would show me that I was pregnant, I felt everything deeply with this baby, she was something different, someone different. She would be someone to come into my world to change me.

As my pregnancy went further along, I hit 20 weeks, and then decided that I didn't just want a midwife, I needed a doula! Someone who could support my decisions and be my voice in that ward when no one else was listening. When I was hitting my limits I needed someone who knew how to talk to the nurses and tell them what I truly wanted.

This was the starting point to reclaiming my power and speaking my truth fully. Saying that I wanted a doula to be with me went against what most people thought was the right thing to do. I had people question whether a doula was qualified, if they would have enough knowledge, if they truly were a support network, plus a lot worse.

Through it all my husband, Gavin, said "alright let's do it." So the hunt for the best doula began, I went completely off feelings as I searched through the people around me that travelled to that area. Then I found the perfect one, who had the values, the vibe and the energy that was my sort of person.

Next was to meet her, just to double check, but really when intuition guides us to people, there is no real mistake on who we find.

So for the next couple of months, I met with her, I went sparingly to the doctors appointments, almost to the point of avoiding them. Only going enough to keep them happy, but with each appointment, each meeting I grew more distant from the mainstream style, and started to turn within asking myself what was needed.

I would start to ask my body and my baby, what is it we need to have today to fuel ourselves? Hearing when I needed rest, and to eat, to dance, to laugh... I started to trust this body that I had, for so long, battled.

The final straw came, I was still doing the doctors appointments, I still was doing the bare minimal blood tests. When it came to the glucose tests, I told them NO. This was the first time I ever let myself say no to someone in this sort of position. For the rebel I was, I still had bowed to these sort of circumstances, the medical world, the "normal"...

Yet now, it changed, the blood tests came back saying that I was low in iron and the doctor told me... "You've got to have an iron infusion!!" There was a deafening roar inside my head, "NOOO! We do NOT need that!"

I started to cry, this was such a big moment for me, a huge moment for me. One I couldn't have really prepared for, I never realised how much doctors, nurses and other medical people thought they had the final say until this point.

I practically begged the doctor to let me have a week, a week to get my levels up in a way that would be sustainable, and for them to be happy with. For them, I shudder now thinking that I was brought to tears thinking that they had such a power over me. But this moment taught me so much that I may never have experienced without it.

In this time I found the answers, I found what my body truly needed. And within the week I had my iron levels up to a satisfactory (according to them) level. Yet my distrust had been set in with outside sources, especially when they still pushed for something I didn't want and that my body didn't need.

One could say this was an awakening on many levels.

It was at this point I decided I was going to birth at home. In the back of my mind, there was a little whisper that spoke and said, "you'll be doing this at home with just your love... And it will be BEAUTIFUL. It will be HEALING! And you won't feel alone, you can trust yourself and your body."

I heard this, but I pursued to find a homebirth midwife... This was at 36 weeks when I started to search. When I found dead ends everywhere. I knew... I knew that I truly was doing this free without anyone bar me, my love, and my babies. At home.

I was calm, I was prepared, and I was happy about it. I started to prod deeper. What would I need? I spoke with my doula, who at this stage had stopped being my official doula, once there was a freebirth because for her it just couldn't happen. I was okay with that, all I needed now was the birthing space to be prepared, and stupidly against my own judgement, I thought I needed someone to look after the kids.

That one decision led to fear being whispered to me, as the one I asked to watch the kids sat in her own fear. This led to discussions that at first created fear in my own mind until I felt into this moment, and realised then that not everyone will approve of what our decisions are, often for their own fear, their own disconnection to their intuition and their own disempowered themes. With that, I was able to be okay with her fear, let it go and embrace what my next step of the journey was to be.

What a space it was to be, collecting the ingredients to this next step of my journey, to be speaking through my own intuition, rather than being kept stuck in what another thought was best.

I knew I was going to have a water birth, so a birthing pool was a must. I sought out crystals that brought the energies I was after. I created the space that I needed to feel completely present and in my own body during this transition.

Not just from maiden to mother, because this truly was my fourth motherhood step. No this time it was blossoming from mother to goddess... the warrior, the goddess, and the most empowered version of self being uplifted for this time. This time I was tuning into the wisdoms of those who had gone before me. Into the spirit and soul of my soon to be born child. And into my own soul, finally feeling her in her essences.

I stopped counting the days, knowing my baby wasn't going to be here on the expected date, I knew she had longer to grow with me before birthing her to the world. So I stayed comfortable and knowing that it would happen exactly when it was needed to happen.

Around me the world went on, I stopped attending the maternity appointments, I stopped creating space for those who felt fear.

I spoke kindness into my soul. I shared wisdoms with my husband. I leant into knowing that my three babies wouldn't be in the space. So it was going to be all around me, my breath. My husband and his energy and the beauty ready to be birthed into this world.

The day started off and I knew it was the day, the one that my body and soul had been preparing for. This was the day I got to speak from intuition. Whenever fear crept forward, love ran beside me and reminded me that it was okay.

I asked for warmth, for calm and for stillness. I swayed through the day and breathed through the waves. The mild contractions coming and going. And the whispers of my soul speaking to me as I then shared everything with my husband on what was going on for me. I kept in contact with my friend and doula letting her know that it was going to be today, that our little one was going to be born.

As the day went on, we hit early night and everything stopped, I asked and turned inside, why have we stopped, why is it still. The fear again creeping up, the fear that maybe something was wrong. What if I couldn't trust my own body like I thought I could?

What if I made a grave mistake?

Hush, Mumma, it's quiet time now. Let my siblings rest then we will prepare to meet... There was a knowing wash over that this was divine and perfect. That it was time for all to settle and that when all was settled, we would be ready.

I voice it to Gav, it's calm, it's quiet. The contractions, the surges, they are gone. It is okay though, it's time to rest for now.

I found my spot close to the fire, and played the music. This was the time for quiet, not the time to roar. The time to be present and hearing.

Then as the moonlight rose, and the kids grew quiet, then everything became intense again.

This time I was hurried in my words, knowing that it was time to be truly prepared. Telling my darling husband the whole time exactly what needed to happen. From filling the pool, now, not later now. It's not time to screw around. It's time to get it done.

The contractions came in longer waves, most of the chatter had gone inward now. The speaking was to myself before to the world. As the pool filled, I knew it was time to get in. No, I do not want to wait, I need to get into the pool.

I had the candles lit, the crystals close, a warm pool and allowed the surges to flow through me. Quiet whimpers at first turned to roars. Breathing, connecting and understanding each piece.

I spoke the wisdom that I was getting to Gavin. I told him each step of the way. Allowing him to know, between each contraction, and then to that moment, her head is birthing now.

I stood alone in the birth pool, untouched and unphased by the world around me, going deep inside, allowing the births of before this to be rewritten, the unheard version of me to finally stand up and be heard by all.

And as with the birth of my daughter into the pool, there now stood the rebirthed version of me. Not just a Mumma, not just a birthing person. But the full version of me, the one now realising her power and what I was capable of... When I tuned in and connected with my own heart and soul.

My daughter was born on the full moon and met first by her father who pulled her from the water, and then placed into my arms. My little Selene, the moon goddess, born shifting the world before even opening her eyes.

I stood strong for this birth, for me, for her, and for the power of women. I freebirthed my daughter after not being heard, after not speaking my truth after not being strong, and not taking courage before.

It took feeling stripped of my voice to turn within and ask myself, speak with myself, to then be able to speak outward. To have the shaky voice at first, to have the tears flood my eyes, to turn to others for advice, and then realise that I had the knowing all along.

The same knowing that would give me the voice to share each step of my wild birth. To be able to then keep standing sovereign and speaking my truth from that moment on.

Birth can look like many different things, from the physical birth, to bringing to the world a new creation. And in all birth, we as the creators, the creatrix, and creatress of our world get to stand up and speak strongly for what our inner knowing truly is.

Creation is one of the biggest pieces that gives us our power back, we get to speak our truth. We get to turn within and listen to what's inside that needs to be brought out.

For me, this birth, the creation of another one of my beautiful children, was a turning point. I didn't realise how powerful I could truly be. I had been reliant on others to tell me what I needed to do, how I needed to do it. Even when there was an inner voice telling me NO. I went against myself for far too long.

It may be something as simple as being told that I need to have an iron infusion, but it was the final straw over an accumulation of being told what I was meant to do, going directly against my own knowledge, inner wisdom, and innate beautiful intuition.

I seek to you, don't let it get to the final straw, don't let it be that moment of breakdown before hearing the wisdom within. Before sharing your voice. The world is ready, always, for more authentic beauties being able to share their voice for themselves.

Give yourself the permission to create freely from your own beautiful essence. Being rebirthed into the energy that is yours, rather than the words of others.

And with that intuition, speak, speak your inner truth to the outer world. Speak to your inner voice, acknowledge, understand, hear her in all her gloriousness.

Shed, let go and be willing to go against the fear of others. They may not understand what you are doing, or why, until it's done.

My beautiful friend, I saw her the day after I had my Selene, and she apologized when that moment happened. She spoke of her fear, and then she saw the power that it had for me and for herself. In me continuing and still pursuing the truth for myself, and pursuing my beliefs, what I needed... It gave her permission to let go of her fear she had around trusting herself. It gave her the moment of acknowledging that fear was there and she came to forgive herself for actions in her life that she didn't stand strong when she wished she did.

It all comes into a beautiful circle, much like the circles held for women, under the full moons... When we speak our truths, share our wisdoms, and trust our intuition on what we are being guided to do we then create something greater, we birth in a way that we may never have seen ourselves birthing.

Since then, I have been able to use this piece of myself to share who I am, and come into a greater understanding of myself. It doesn't just end with one time and that's it either. Once we find our voices, find our authentic soul calling through us, we get to keep going strong.

Now, I have had another freebirth, wild and sovereign and let my rebel heart fly strong. Through this one day, one birthing experience I healed a wounding that had me fighting myself.

This has become my purpose in life, to empower other women, mothers, those who have had their voices squashed and denied themselves permission to speak loudly and authentically. I stand for them, as I share each day snippets of life, the ups, the downs and the rounds and rounds. I share circle for women every month by the full moon, not just because of its beautiful energy but because for me it was a turning point in who I was.

I am now showing these women, these mothers, that raising your voice doesn't end in pain, it doesn't mean that you are creating trouble. No, it's honouring your soul, your purpose, and when we do this in our most authentic way we can find the opportunities that we may have missed out on previously that will start to flood us with an abundant life.

I want to end this by really sharing with you, don't be put off by me speaking only of birth, as I spoke creation on all levels takes bravery, takes courage and is love in action. Do what you love, for you, for that voice. Allow it to roar when you need to, be still when calm is asked for. Turn within to speak without...

And if you are a Mumma pregnant, and wanting to take the path of your own voice, there are many women that can support you, hold space for you, and you Mumma, you have your own wisdom deep within you, trust and it will share with you all you need to know.

KALI J WALTERS

After living a life of abuse and trauma in her childhood, Kali J fell into the state of addiction and repeating the cycles she saw before her. Kali J found her way out of it all by saying enough was enough and created differently in her life.

Now, Kali J is a mother to five, more than that, she is embracing all parts of her wild, free, fun, and adventurous spirit that had been squashed years ago. Kali J now uses her journey to be the permission slip for other Mummas to move from the role they play to their truth.

Kali J is the founder of The Mummas Permission Movement, a space for mothers to show up authentically, relearn how to create the lifestyle they desire through personal development and learning new skills. Kali J knows village is important and holds monthly Full Moon Mummas Circles for all to join!

Kali J would love to have you connect with her at:
Website: http://kalijwalters.com
Facebook: www.facebook.com/KaliJWalters55
The Mummas Permission Movement:
www.facebook.com/groups/mpmovement/

17

CAROLINE WONG

FINDING TRUE NORTH

I am not supposed to be here. Well, that is according to the doctor that delivered me days after I was born. Due to the fact that I was born without enzymes, I was not able to hold any nutrients in my body, therefore starving to death. Because my body was fighting for it's life, my heart was racing out of control. The doctor alluded to the fact that I had exceeded the amount of digitalis (medication to slow the heart rate down) and my heart could not take anymore. It would be about a day or so and I would basically give myself a heart attack based on the condition I was in. This was how I spent my first weeks on Earth, clinging to life and not even aware of it. To make a long story short, a doctor created a formula that saved me.

You are probably thinking, this is a book of speaking intuitive truth, how is this the story? Looking back on childhood memories, I don't have a lot of vivid experiences to speak of, but there is one that has stuck with me. Each Christmas, my parents would throw these large holiday parties. I would be excited about the red and green bread, getting to eat the celery pieces as my dad meticulously cut them for the hors d'oeuvres platters and sneaking a few of the gourmet cookies before the guests arrived. This is how my fascination with the ethereal and unexplainable dreams came to be.

I repeatedly had a dream as a kid in which the room is completely white and I am standing in the middle. I can't tell where it begins or ends. Actually, it was kind of scary for me. During the party, my parents would take people on a tour of our home. It was a pretty cool house. The master bathroom was huge and kind of swank by Elle Decor standards . Black sinks, tub, shower, gold fixtures, marble, mirrors, etc. Somehow, I must have gotten left behind on one of the tours.

I sat on the bathroom counter and this woman was there. I could see myself in multiple mirrors and it was oddly the same feeling I got in the dream of the white space, except things were black. This woman begins to ask me if I had dreams I could not explain? You can imagine, I was only about five at the time. Why would she be asking me this? I assume she is referring to the white space dreams? How does she know about my all white space dreams? Am I really experiencing this?

The woman proceeds to tell me that I am here to do something big but it will not be for a long time and to not be afraid of the dreams that take me to the white space. I'm not sure how she was expecting me to process that, but it left me confused for a really long time. According to her, there was something different about me. Note at the time I had no idea about how I came fighting into this world.

After the party I described this lady to my mom and dad and they had no answers. That was my first encounter with the unexplainable in real-time. At what point does the brain understand the concept of intuition? How are we aware that something is going to happen? As children, unless someone is speaking the concept of intuition to us, it is essentially a foreign concept.

Childhood memories that I do have after that incident were mainly of my sister and I being taken to other relatives' houses or family friends. You don't really question it because you have nothing to compare it to. I can say though, that when we were at home, there was frequent turmoil.

Fast forward to when I am eleven years old. I began to get sick a lot, I was in and out of the hospital frequently. One of my hospital stays was for two and a half months. I was placed on a feeding tube because I had lost so much weight. They put the tube in with the hopes I would gain weight. It didn't work. This all took place in about a year's time. That year, it was like I was slowly dying. Different from how I began life, quickly dying. My body began to poison itself from the amount of infection that it was suffering. The last gastro-intestinal specialist determined that I would need surgery. My system had gone septic. Honestly, I didn't think that I was going to come out of that surgery.

With my stuffed animal smurf in my arms, they wheeled me off to no coincidence, a cold white room. This time it was not a dream. I had never seen an O.R. before. The white space and bright lights chillingly reminded me of that dream. No intuition of what was to come, just a blank stare at the ceiling. My last conversation was with the anesthesiologist, I asked if my smurf could stay with me during surgery. He said of course and then I remember nothing else.

Approximately nine hours later, I woke up with a smurf stuffed animal in my hands just as I requested and in a great deal of pain. I was saved again. When I was laying there that night in the hospital, watching the nurse switch my blood transfusion bags, I thought back to the conversation with the woman who has no name. Clearly she had no idea what she was talking about. At this point I was aware of the birth story because of all of the doctors visits.

I ended up being diagnosed with Crohn's disease, which didn't paint a pretty picture for me as a kid. I thought to myself, "if I'm so special how am I laying here feeling half dead?" Is this the special part of my life she was talking about?

Believe me, I wasn't thinking anything amazing. To be honest, I wasn't sure if I would be able to make it through the recovery. I remember it being painful and very hard. And, as an almost 12- year-old, I had no prior experience in this area.

So, can the body intuitively heal itself? I did not know a thing about intuition but what I kept clinging onto was what this woman had said to me. I ended up healing and by the grace of God, was not the typical Crohn's patient. The doctors that operated on me were mesmerized at my recovery and every check-up ended up with high fives and a "you're something special kid" before I walked out the door.

I went on to have about three more incidents that I probably shouldn't have survived. Maybe those stories will surface at some point but I want to explain the truth I have learned from these initial ones moving forward.

After having been in situations where I did not have the ability to speak my truth or harness intuition, I now believe it was my soul speaking and doing the survival chats for me. How else can I explain it? Back then I knew nothing of hypnotherapy, yoga, crystals, energy healing, etc. I didn't know about intuition and speaking up for myself. Maybe what the truth is, is that the contract we have with our soul knows when we are ready to have the curtains pulled back. It becomes our choice in how we process intuition from there. As I look back, I don't even think I prayed for myself when I went into surgery, but I am assuming someone else did.

After everything that I have learned, I am convinced that these experiences teach us to listen carefully to the quiet whispers of the soul. My soul releases things to me as she feels I can handle them. The last ten years have proven to me that learning how to read, cultivate, and nurture my intuition has resulted in a metamorphosis.

Intuition is hard to sell because you can't see it. You have to feel it. When you are not in touch with your body, how could you feel it?

What do you even begin to look for? Where do you even go looking for it? How do you believe in it? Is it even real? If you believe in God or a form of spirituality why isn't that enough? These are all questions I began asking myself and the quest began.

My soul began to slowly teach me and allow me to feel intuitively in the darkness of my own cocoon. When she knew I was ready to follow and speak my truth, she gave me wings. Emerging from the cocoon, she opened up my book of life and began to illuminate the way.

As I write this story, tears run down my face. I have realized that I was never alone. It was going to happen this way all along. The timing of the experiences in the last ten years all lead to these revelations and sharing my truths. It seemed like I was in the dark a lot, questioning, examining situations, healing from more medical things, losing my father, and one of my best friends, raising kids, moving to another city, etc., the growing pains of life. But the difference it made this time was that I now had tools to move through these rocks that were on the path. Some of them felt like boulders but I forged on and although I could not see my own wings, they were there carrying me beautifully.

So now what? Where does this lead me?

One of the intuitive nudges I followed was hypnotherapy and that was the true catalyst of change. I found hypnotherapy as I was looking for something to shift my mindset. Yoga was great for the physical release of emotions and trauma but I needed something to help the endless negative loops inside my thoughts. At that point, my intuition was much better honed and I recognized more readily when my soul was leaning in and whispering to me. After a few pre-recorded hypnosis sessions, I was sold. I needed to be certified so that I could bring this to other people and help them.

Attending the first weekend-long training was the first time I experienced an in-person session. It was like time stood still. In moments of practice, I could see myself shift and change. Parts were surreal. Unless you experience hypnotherapy, it's hard to fairly justify.

My world has changed since opening up to this practice. The more I allowed change, old patterns fell away and the intuitive part of me has continued to flourish. She now trusts with certainty and conviction when she believes in something. No longer doubting her worthiness. She understands how this directly affects her ecosystem and perseveres to embrace her gifts so they can be shared with the world.

Speaking my truth is without reservation. I realize that I am not doing any justice to myself or the planet by not speaking up. Sharing stories of how I beat the odds and watched the phoenix rise within, are real stories. It is experience and learned wisdom. If I kept it to myself, how could I help others to see the same beauty and gifts within themselves?

Speaking my truth is no longer an option. My daughters have witnessed this transformation. I am teaching them what the gift of intuition brings and how they too learn the significance in speaking their own truths. What an amazing experience to watch. It is a blessing for me to see this in them.

I don't want to leave any stone unturned. The legacy I leave will be that I helped others find that courageous and unapologetically intuitive soul within.

If we do not share these lessons, some will go into the world needlessly suffering, using the wrong band-aids to heal their wounds and wander through without purpose and conviction.

In speaking my truth, I am humbled that I can share a glimpse of my story assuring someone that they are not alone. The key though is that they have to want the change.

As intuition and speaking our truth continues to make ripples in the ethers, we pave the way for generations to come to lessen their suffering and instead be courageous and unapologetic with their actions.

Intuition is felt in the frequency and soul of our being. Navigating the soul from that space will be an adventure.

I guess the moral of my story is, life will have ups and downs. Learn how to be in touch with your intuition and believe her when she speaks. Trust her motives and know that when we are incapable of knowing the next step, God, spirit, etc. steps in and takes the wheel. You are exactly where you need to be.

As for doing something big in life like the lady said I would do... Those words carried me through lots of uncertain times. I think I get it now. Learning to be your amazing self is the biggest thing you can do in life and then share that with the world. If you feel that you've fallen down a rabbit hole you aren't having luck getting out of, here are some lessons I've learned;

1. Wherever you are, take an inventory, write it all out and then sit with it. Some situations will be more uncomfortable than others, but stay with the thoughts. What are they telling you? Is it asking you to do anything? What are you learning from this? Have you been here before? If yes, why do you think you are back again? What is your inner wisdom asking you to do? Journal until it is all out. When you feel like you are done journaling, close your eyes and take several deep breaths. If it produces tears, anger, frustration, let it out. When you are ready, go back and look at what you wrote to yourself. Use this strategy when you need direction.

2. Remember that your negative thoughts about yourself are not 100% real. What do I mean? Negative talk keeps you in sabotage mode. It's a comfort zone that the brain is ok with. It is safe. You are less likely to help yourself or try new things when you don't believe it will work. For example, if someone said to themselves, "I am

overweight and no one will ever love me and I will be stuck like this forever." That is negative talk and self-sabotage. If you stay in that place, you will keep complaining and be unhappy potentially but the brain thinks it's saving you from getting your heart broken, so negative talk becomes a safe place. By learning how to reduce negative talk and sabotage, inner guidance becomes stronger and you will lessen the amount of chatter in negative land. This opens up happier neural pathways that will actually create responses to change your habits for the better.

3. Learn how your body feels when something is a yes or no intuitively. This may take a few tries but you will get the hang of it. Close your eyes and ask yourself a question. When you get the answer to it, see how your body feels. If it is a yes and feels good, what does the body feel like? If it is a no and the body has a reaction, where are you feeling it? Where do you feel the shift in the body? Is anything physically hurting, ex: stomach hurts all of the sudden, lump in your throat, headache, pain in your neck, etc. These are indicators that your body isn't trusting or not happy with a decision or situation. So, the next time you are in a situation you are unsure of, ask the body how it feels. It will take some time to become insync with your decisions but it is a good place to start.

4. Believe that you have the innate power to change your path if you are not happy with the one you are on. You need to be present and aware of signs, messages, and that soul wisdom space that makes suggestions to you from time to time. Settling is a conditioned response due to thought patterns we have learned from birth. As we get older, we just buy into the fact that this is the way it is until it isn't. The more you begin to loosen the reins fear has on your decision making, you open the door to trusting your own intuition and allowing her own truth to speak openly

5. Nothing changes if nothing changes. You can sit and wonder why, how, not again, etc. or you can do something about it. Stop reacting to what life deals you and be proactive with what you do with your

life. No more excuses, no more living in the pain-body, no more saying, "I will do this tomorrow...". You may never get that chance. Every day that we wake up and take a breath is a gift. I know. It's so cliche, but true. Be the thing you want the most of, that version of you that you long for. Be her, because by being her in your mind, you realize what it will take to get there, and you begin to do those things and have those experiences. The same will only produce the same. Small changes over time will result in big gains but you have to make the move.

My wish for you is to love yourself fiercely. Be your own advocate. Go after those crazy dreams that scare you. Feed yourself with beautiful words. Make power moves. If your crown tilts, straighten it and walk taller. Step into your power and don't give it up. Have compassion for others, for you don't know the path they have had to walk. Donate your time. Listen to others intently. Believe we can all sit at the abundant table. Do more yoga. Meditate daily. Drink water. Drown your woes in sweat. Sit under the moon. Bathe in the sea. Look at the clouds in wonderment. Don't just tell someone you love them, show them. Laugh daily. Move your body. Write love notes to yourself and others. Be unapologetically yourself because everyone else is taken. You rock. Lastly, let your truth speak intuitively, fiercely, and with love.

CAROLINE WONG

Caroline Wong is a hypnotherapist, 500RYT yoga instructor, and a business energy advisor. She is passionate about teaching women how to change the way they look at life by cultivating meaningful mindset shifts while harnessing their energy through yoga, meditation, and breathwork. Lastly, Caroline teaches them how to use crystal energy to balance their home, work, and personal life. She has a signature course Just Add Water which can be found on the website. Teaching women to stand in their power, unapologetically as themselves is Caroline's way of cultivating an energetic can-do road map for the new age woman who is here to blaze a trail. Also leaving an impact on the lives of our youth by spreading yoga and mindfulness in schools.

She is the creator of Tru North Tribe and the podcast Tried and Tru, co-author of Intutive, Speaking her Truth, and an Executive Writer for Brainz Magazine.

Website: www.thetrunorthtribe.com
Podcast: www.anchor.fm/caroline-wong

18

AUDRA GORDON

TRUTH BE TOLD

*T*here are those who are afraid of the unknown and then there are those who embrace it. If you were told to keep a secret, could you? I was born seeing through the veil. I've been able to see heaven from an early age, communicate with loved ones who have passed on, and see angels in different forms. Visiting with them was my escape and my greatest secret. Not only was this my hidden gift, but my children's as well, because they had inherited my peculiar strengths. The time came when we needed to be our authentic selves and allow our experiences to unfold naturally without fear and judgment. The day I exposed everything was when the silence finally ended.

My truth started back when I was young in a small town in northern California where I grew up with my older sister and identical twin. My twin sister and I did everything together and were inseparable. We knew everything about each other and what we were doing even if we weren't in the same location. We had such a tight bond that we felt each other all of the time. We knew what each other was thinking, and spoke to each other telepathically often which was something that we had started doing before we were born. It was so natural to us that there were times we would communicate this way without realizing it.

I was pretty young when I started noticing that having that ability, among others, wasn't the norm for people. It didn't sit well with my mother either and from an early age, I was instructed to never tell anyone outside of our family what I was able to do. Everything that involved my abilities moving forward was held in secrecy. But even with this restriction in place, it didn't prevent things from happening as I didn't have control over when or where it would reveal itself.

Many times spirits and angels would engage in conversation with me and show me things that blew my mind. I had a strong feeling about places and people and knew things that no one had shared with me. In a way, life was magical because I could instinctively feel nature by its touch; the trees and buildings had stories to tell, objects I held would share its' history, and being in certain places would reveal the emotional temperature of the people who had been there. I would see aura's as I walked past people with spirits mixed in with them as they carried on with their day, oblivious that they weren't alone. One ability I loved most was knowing when things were going to happen before they came to be. Most of the time it would be little things like knowing who was calling before the phone rang, who was at the front door and I'd see detailed conversations appear in my mind like a video clip. In fact, this is how I knew that we were adopted by my stepfather, but most things I saw weren't about me, it was about other people, and not everything was what I wanted to see.

A majority of the things that I was able to do happened on their own without me trying to make it work, but there were also many days where nothing happened at all. On the days that I was feeling bored, curiosity would get the best of me and I would create new things to try with my abilities to see if it would work. I had many failed attempts with some pretty crazy ideas but one thing I tried ended up working that got me excited. I was in the second grade when I was sitting at my desk that was located by a wall of windows. Hanging in front of them was a mobile that the teacher had made from small wooden dowels and string that hung 6 owls cut from construction paper. As the wind gently came into the room the owls would slowly turn in circles. I remember thinking to myself that I wanted the lower right owl to stop moving so I told it to stop in my mind, and it did! Thinking that this was likely a fluke, I tried it again with the lower-left owl this time and it also worked! I felt like my hands were directing the movement through my gaze, which didn't make sense to me but I knew that I was somehow controlling it. Over the next few weeks, I kept upping the challenge by picking specific owls to circle one way, while the others circled the opposite, and I'd make some of the owls move while stopping the rest, or make a circle faster than the others, and without fail, it would happen every time I maintained my focus.

This began my journey moving objects through intention and more importantly, fueled my belief that I was capable of doing things that otherwise seemed impossible. Thirty years went by before I knew that this technique was referred to as Telekinesis back in 1890 by Russian researcher and author, Alexander N. Aksakof. I love telling this story because this experience has greatly influenced my approach with mediumship and how I teach. When I was moving the owls, I didn't have anyone over my shoulder discouraging me from trying to do something that was "out there" or tell me that I couldn't do it. I truly believed that I could, and that belief is what made it so. It had a profound effect on me because it showed me that we have a much farther ethereal reach than we realize, and we're more powerful than we can ever imagine. Our bodies are made of energy, as are our thoughts and our words. What we believe and put our energy into, is our reality, and our reality is limitless if we trust and have discipline. This concept propelled my mediumship to a level that surpassed all expectations I had and was what separated me from being average to exceptional in my reach.

After high school, I married and worked various corporate jobs that provided stability and great experiences, but nothing compared to being a mom. The time came when I was able to change roles and be home full-time to be with my children, which filled my heart with so much joy. To this day I don't think they ever knew how captivated I was by them when they were young. I watched their every move hoping to engrain those memories into my head forever. I would watch them sleep, play, eat, giggle - everything. Those moments are so precious to me and my love and respect for them are beyond measure. During this time I was also able to sit back and watch their abilities unfold which was quite a sight to see as well. All three of them are strong empaths, have been able to see and communicate with spirits, and are very intuitive. They also have abilities unique to them as individuals. My oldest daughter has the keen ability to read and work with animals and to energetically heal and predict future events. My second daughter can read people like the back of her hand and can energetically heal others as well. Her intuition and psychic senses are amazingly accurate. My son can perform remote viewing, predict future events, and know things without being privy to the information beforehand. I treasure how they embraced who they were and accepted their gifts so easily.

At the time my children were young, people still weren't ready to accept anyone into their lives that were gifted, and just as my mother had done with me, I asked my children not to share that they could do all of these amazing things with their friends but allowed them to share it when they were old enough to answer questions on their own and explain things with maturity. Thankfully, they were ok with this and didn't mind keeping their secret until they were ready. Until then, they were free to be themselves at home and because I was a gifted child at one time and knew what it was like to be in their shoes, I was able to give them support and encouragement that allowed their gifts to blossom in a natural and healthy way. This experience also enables me to counsel other parents who are in need of guidance for their gifted children and has become a special focus of mine through the years to mentor children who are growing into their life enhanced with the ability to see, hear and feel energy and spirits around them.

I'll admit, seeing my children honing in on their abilities reminded me of my childhood and I began to miss the gifts that I had put aside once life got busy. I asked God to give me signs of what I was to do next and if my gifts were to be a part of my life's purpose. Within a few weeks, I found myself on a popular social media platform when I discovered a group in my newsfeed that allowed people to ask questions and anyone could answer them. As I thumbed through the questions and shared my responses I learned how much it was helping people. It quickly turned into a nightly event after my children went to sleep, and I'd spend hours reading for people. Before I knew it I was working with law enforcement on missing person cases and discovering new niches with my mediumship. This inspired me to start reading animals, working with psychometry more and reading objects, performing body scans and learning how to do health readings, and even delved into past life readings to see how they intertwined with unexplained fears and phobias that we experience in this lifetime. To say that I was enjoying the process of my development is an understatement!

After a couple of years working in various groups, I started my own group called Lifting The Psychic Veil that provides members with a safe place to be read and receive guidance when they're in need of answers or if they're wanting to connect with loved ones in spirit. The group also provides a space for members to practice giving readings to strengthen their efforts in psychic and mediumship unfoldment, participate in intuitive exercises to elevate their vibrational frequencies, and engage in Q&A sessions. As the group continued to grow, and more people were coming in at different points of their journey, I needed to find a way to expand on the mechanics of mediumship that was geared towards an individual's understanding and level of ability. I soon launched a development course and mentorship program that is specifically designed for each person who takes it so that they have the tools they need to succeed, whether they're new to mediumship or want to level up. Once I did this, I finally felt that I could teach in a relatable way that was down to earth and easy to understand.

As the group began gaining traction, I was finding my voice and becoming more comfortable sharing my life-long secret with those who also embraced their spirituality. During this process, I knew that if I wanted to forge ahead in this field I needed to break down more barriers that I had put up through the years and feel free to talk about this outside of my group without feeling so vulnerable. One afternoon I mustered up the courage to let my friends and acquaintances know who I was and what I was about. I was so nervous I didn't know what to say, so I sat down at my computer and began typing the words, "I was born a Medium", and let the rest of the words flow naturally across the screen. As I finished typing my story, I hit enter and the post was live. Eeek! I've never felt more exposed, it was definitely a nail-biting moment. The first few minutes went by as I waited for the responses to come in and surprisingly not one person unfriended me or walked away. There was no criticism, only acceptance. All of that worry I was holding on to for so long was over nothing and I have to say that was the most liberating moment I've ever had! Man did it feel good to get that out of the way! By doing this, I was finally able to live a life of authenticity and be proud of who I was. I didn't have to hide anymore, and to be honest, if someone didn't approve of who I was, I was ok if they didn't want to be in my life anymore because at this point I needed to be surrounded by those who were able to support me and bring positive energy to our relationship. I would recommend to anyone who is thinking about becoming a psychic or medium to consider coming out to those you know early in your journey because lifting this burden will help to open you up more to your guides and spirit allowing your gifts to unfold naturally without blocks or delays. Doing this will bring your walls down which is necessary to connect, and will help you gain confidence in your work.

Looking back at how easy it was unveiling my truth, I often wondered what it would have been like for me had I done this much sooner. It would have made my life so much easier when it came to expressing myself but I have to believe that the timing was meant to be. I grew up in a generation where anyone who had spiritual gifts was feared because there was very little published about the six senses for people to truly understand what they were. Because of this fear of the unknown people were harsh to judge and easily outcasted anyone who observed unique differences that they couldn't understand. They surmised that anyone having these abilities were either Satanists, delusional or schizophrenic. I would hear stories growing up that people were being admitted into the insane asylum for exhibiting their gifts and the shame that followed them was enough to deter me from opening up to people and allowing my children to do the same, but things were starting to change. People were beginning to explore their own spirituality and through that process were naturally expanding their conscious awareness and defining what their new reality of existence was. Knowledge and acceptance began to spread and soon people were seeking out psychics and mediums for guidance at a rate that we've never seen before. A significant number of people began acknowledging that mediumship was making it easier for them to work through the grieving process. I was coming out in a time when people were ready to have guidance in their lives in a way that couldn't be offered by physicians and therapists, and this brought me comfort knowing that divine timing was definitely at play.

Over time, I was getting to know hundreds of people through my group who were either booking psychic readings with me or reaching out eager to pursue their calling as a medium and healer. A common question would always come up in both instances, and people wanted to know why they were living such a challenging life. I think many of us can relate to this. As they shared their stories with me I learned one key element that linked everyone together that seemed to make all of our experiences relevant to who we are. Every encounter that we've gone through, both good and bad, have taught us lessons that were instrumental to our personal growth because they were helping us become stronger and resilient. Once we learn the life lessons behind those experiences we're able to release everything else that isn't serving us. For example, when we feel fear it's teaching us to find our courage, and when we run into a situation that we can't control it's showing us how to let go. When someone is taking their anger out on us it's an opportunity to find compassion for them because their actions are the result of wounds they're suffering from and loving unconditionally permits us to forgive which instills us with peace and understanding. Everything that we've gone through has made us better people because these experiences were aligning us with our life purpose. Looking back, I've never come across a healer or lightworker that hasn't lived a life filled with challenges, compromise, or defeat, and there is good reason for that. For us to help and heal others, we need to be familiar with how those emotions feel to identify what others are going through. This is especially important with empaths because our empathy acts as our internal radar to aid us in recognizing who needs healing and why. So the more experiences we go through, both good and bad, the more effective we're going to be at distinguishing the emotional wounds enabling us to become better psychics and mediums. The universe has been shaping us into becoming healers through our experiences our entire lives. How amazing is that!

It's fair to say that I've learned a lot while maneuvering through my personal journey and finding my place in this world as a healer. My quest to keep evolving will always be a part of who I am. And as a medium, I'm *extremely* happy that I came out in the open and embraced this way of life because I've seen the most miraculous transformations happen during my sessions that I wouldn't have had the pleasure of experiencing any other way. The messages that come from spirit give people courage to move past situations, hope to move forward in life, peace to forgive and let go, and closure to unanswered questions. It is healing people beyond measure and is something that I'm blessed to be a part of. Honestly, I can't imagine living my life any differently.

AUDRA GORDON

Audra Gordon is an International Psychic Medium and is dedicated to bringing the voices of loved ones in spirit alive again through her readings. Her approach is down-to-earth as she moves hearts with detailed messages that heal and provide closure.

Audra is also an Intuitive Mentor who has been teaching the mechanics of mediumship to people around the world. She helps them embrace their intuition and enhance their unique abilities as they explore their connection to the spirit world. She's published several articles that help people understand their gifts, broaden their conscious awareness and elevate their vibrational frequencies to succeed in their spiritual journeys.

As a mother of three gifted children as well as having her own since childhood, she's able to assist parents and children, providing them with guidance and tools that will allow their gifts to flourish in a nurturing and healthy way, by taking the fear out of the unknown.

Website: www.TheAngelsMedium.com
Facebook: www.facebook.com/TheAngelsMedium

19

JO WIEHLER

LIFE IS A BOLD ADVENTURE

*I*t was a beautiful crisp-Autumn type of day, 9/11/2018 to be exact. I was just driving back from JFK Airport, after the tearful trip to drop my beautiful daughter Alex off, where her new adventure awaits! She was on her way to Scotland to work as a nanny for a few months.

After our tearful good-bye, I began my own adventure driving back to my home in Pennsylvania at the very bottom corner of the State. I was excited to take the long scenic route home!

So many hours to think, drive at my leisure, and sightseeing... and yes cry! My precious baby has gone to start her own journey... in Scotland! Was I crazy to let her do this? Was I a bad mom? What was I thinking to have agreed to this? My Momma-brain took me in all kinds of directions.

STOP!!!

"You, Jo Wiehler, have taught your daughter to boldly, passionately, and fearlessly go forward in the directions of her dreams! That life is a bold and daring adventure or nothing at all."

Breathe! ...BREATHE!!! "She is a smart, incredible, brilliant, beautiful young woman, and a Capricorn! And one heck of a sharpshooter." I laughed! She will be fine.

With this self-talk going on, I pulled over to say a prayer, and put my greatest gift back in the hands of the good Lord, "Please protect her, and take care of her! If not you will have to deal with me...the Momma-Bear!" (I might have put that threat out there- just in case!) Looking at my phone to see if there were any more text messages from her. "Oh yeah! Three messages!"

First one ... "MOM! BREATHE!!! ...I'M FINE! ...RELAX!!! BREATHE"

Second one ... "I love you"

Third one... "Ciao! Buongiorno Jo! My name is Sergio from Italy, we have been told about you by a friend, and we think you are the right lady to buy our house in Italy. Please call me at your fastest time. My WhatsApp is+39 465.46... many kisses. Ciao e tutti Sergio"

What? I don't know anyone in Italy! What is "WhatsApp?" ...Sergio? Who names their kid "Sergio?" Maybe he is in the mafia? I did date that guy all those years ago when I was a nanny in NJ ... he was Italian...but that was when I was 17... I am a bit older now. Who is this? ITALY?

I read this text repeatedly, at every pit stop. Italy? Sergio? As I read this, I felt a very strong burning in my heart, a very warm peaceful feeling came over me, a feeling of right and certainty, and truth. There was such a strong powerful burning feeling that this was right, and more importantly that I was moving to Italy. That this was undeniably right! I was excited, nervous, terrified, and surprisingly calm and peaceful!

WHAT? I DON'T SPEAK ITALIAN...I EAT ITALIAN, THAT WAS AS FLUENT AS I GET!

ITALY???

I pulled in front of my home, tired and just in time to receive the call that my daughter had arrived safely and was with the family. WHEW! She was exhausted and going to sleep! Me too! I took my suitcase upstairs and went to go to sleep. "Ring... Ring... Ring..." I answered it expecting to hear my lovely daughters voice "Hello Honey..." it wasn't my daughter, a very strong Italian accented man cleared his throat, and said in very broken English voice "**My Name is Sergio...**"

I was fully awake at this point!

He proceeded to tell me that he had been told about me from his cousin in Switzerland, (Stefania, I didn't know her either) who had been told by a friend that there was this courageous woman who had a great vision and business mind that I was the right person for their family home, in a town called "Sabbioneta"

I need a map. Sabb-u-what? Where is this place? Maybe it's in Rome, or Venice? I was in a daze, this felt like a dream. Me? Italy? How? I reluctantly gave him my email and told him I had just returned home from a very long drive. I wished him goodnight, with the promise to look it over in the morning. I prayed that my daughter was safe, and that what opportunities he had for me were the right ones and I would know it. Weirdly enough, Italy felt oddly calm and soothing when I said it. As I drifted off to sleep, a nice peaceful feeling, of this beautiful country that I had dreamed about since I was a little girl, but have never thought it would or could become a reality to me and my simple life.

The next day was a busy Wednesday back to work. I was tired, sluggish, and luckily was an outside industrial lighting sales rep. I had booked my appointments, close to home so I didn't have to leave so early. I had completely forgotten about the conversation from the night before.I sent my daughter a message for the day, and was getting used to this new normal of her presence not being there. That week, I worked hard, sold lots of lighting to my customers, warehouses, and nearby business, and even though it was a 3-day workweek for me, it ended up being a very positive one financially for me in sales, and commissions...a very profitable week! But everywhere I went there was some sort of sign, or nudge to Italy!

A lot of my customers, had previously bought their steel buildings from me. Oh yes, I had sold industrial steel buildings, large ones, warehouses, airplane hangers, storage units. No matter what the size building I sold it, and then transitioned into industrial lighting...you know streetlights, airport lights? I love a challenge, and there were also the bigger commission opportunities. They never expected a redheaded lady named "Jo" to show up with a smile. My name in itself got me into many doors, thinking it was "**JOE WIEHLER**", not "**JO WIEHLER**". They never expected to find a beautiful woman behind the name, who was very knowledgeable about the products, services, or buildings. I made a friend first, had them relaxed, and laughing and was welcome through the "back door". I sold more lights and very quickly rose to the #1 sales position in the company.

My goals were to financially make enough that I could work 2-3 days a week and have the money and freedom to do what I chose to. So, the more I sold, the more I made, and the more freedom I created for myself! This plan was working very nicely at this point of my life! All was well in my little world. Since coming home, I had completely forgot about the email. I didn't check my personal email until Sunday! So, when I did, I was in for a nice surprise! The email was from Italy, and whomever this Sergio was! 72 pictures, and description all in Italian! At first look, I hated it! This was definitely not love at first sight, it was more like ... "Ummm...No Thank You!"

But as I was scrolling through the pictures, the thought came to me that this was a massive building (900square meters) which is 10,000 square feet, wow! 9 bedrooms! I come from a very large family and I have always wanted to have all of my family with me. This would be perfect! I love antiques, and the furniture was included...another wow! The price was amazing!

And then my sacred dream came whirling back! My dream that I had put on the shelves for almost 26 years, for many painful reasons, "Jo this could be your B&B!!!"

And with that thought my heart burned, and I felt a strong and powerful whisper that this was my home that the Lord was giving to me! That is when I fell in love. As I was thinking about this, I heard a small voice which scared me even more **"Jo, this is where I need you!"** Have you ever had that voice? So quiet, small, and peacefully, and said with a truth that you can feel in your heart, but also filled with so much strength power and surety, that cannot be denied! That is what scared me the most! From that moment forward all I could do was think about Italy, nonstop! I just decided to go all in and believe it and go on faith and manifesting this into reality! To believe in the grace of God and his mighty hand and miracles! To take the courage to trust!

You see it got to the point that this journey was more than a house in Italy, this was my chance to show the Lord many things. That I believed in Him. That I would act in faith, and that I loved him enough to serve and follow Him. Not my will, but thy will be done. To say in fact...HERE I AM! But let me share a warning, **FAITH IS NOT EASY!!!** Sometimes it's hard work, especially when nobody else can see or hear the vision that you were personally were given. God has his reasons!

"Sometimes Faith will make you look stupid, and then it starts to rain, Noah"

Weeks went by, a few more phone calls back and forth to Italy, many sales coming in, like a bountiful harvest, and the surety kept getting stronger by the day!

October 14, 2018. Up to this date I had not said one word to anyone about this home, or Italy! It was my little secret! It was like being pregnant. The special time that you have just you, and the baby! Sergio asked if I was serious-if I wanted to buy the home. I was scared! I was nervous, I didn't have the courage to say yes. I wanted to vomit! And out of nowhere...I said the loudest most confident, calmest **"Yes"** I have ever said, and accepted the terms, and made plans to come to Italy to sign the paperwork and make the down payment...without seeing the home...and to transfer the money! We got off the phone, I dropped to my knees and said a prayer to the Lord... I was shaking! I have never been so scared in my life. I was crying and prayed my guts out. And then ran to the bathroom and vomited! I was just kidding! I can't do this! I had my fingers crossed! ...But there by the grace of God Go I!

Now to tell my daughter...eek! Once I did, we talked. I respect her ideas, voice and thoughts-she is my voice of reason in any, and all business decisions. "This is going to be like a holiday home," I said "we can go to Italy for the summer, and Christmases, or whenever we can, it will be exciting." With that being said, **God sometimes has other plans!** I received a very strong personal confirmation that I was going to be moving to Italy within this year, as well as all living hell was about to break loose in my life...

I worked up to the 22nd of December, achieving my goals, among the top in sales, commissions, and bonuses were incredible! I was flourishing in all areas! So, I booked a flight to be with my daughter for Christmas and took 3 weeks off, enough time to get a situation sorted. We rented an apartment above a pub and had the most fabulous time for the three weeks. Our "Scottish Christmas" will be one of my favorites. We said our tearful goodbyes again, with plans firmly intact to meet in Italy, to see the home, at the end of February, and to sign the papers. Then I left to come back home!

January 10th, 2019. Upon going through customs in Dublin Airport, I was next in line to go through, and as I waited, I heard a very quiet still voice again "**I need you in Italy, and it starts NOW!**" I was shocked, what did I just hear? I had no time to comprehend what I just heard, as I was called next to go speak with the customs agents. They were two cheerful, beautiful ladies, even wishing me "Happy New Year". As I walked through, they called me back, asked for my passport, and re-stamped it and signed it. "Oh, what does this mean?" I asked. They said sweetly that my alien residency was expiring, and I had until the 8th of July 2020 to leave the country. That I could no longer live, work, or reside, own a home, or business in the United States, and again they wished me a Happy New Year. I had no time to think or process this as I had to run to catch my flight back home.

The following Monday was back to work for me, after three weeks of not working, and the money used for the trip, had left little to nothing in my pockets. So, I hit the pavement, and hit it hard, sale after sale came in, especially the really big one that I had been working on for months!!! $40,000+ sale! That was the best way to end this week!

As well as working my part-time job in the evenings, when you work straight commission, you blanket yourself for times with no sales. I was tired and jet-lagged, and a very long drive back from Philadelphia to my home. I was ready to sleep. I came home early Sunday night from work, soaked up the magic of my beautiful Christmas home, each room lovingly decorated and a total of 35 Christmas trees... I believe go big or go home! I went to sleep around 7:30-8 pm.

My alarm went off and I snoozed a few times, to the last possible minute, and got out of bed...slosh! I stepped into a 5 inch deep puddle of icy cold water! What? What had happened? As I opened my bedroom door, I was horrified to see water gushing down the stairs like a waterfall, shocked to find out that all my pipes had frozen overnight, and burst. The water had been running for about 8-10 hours!

It looked like someone had turned a firehose on in full throttle. I got downstairs, my home was completely flooded. It looked like a lake, ceilings had fallen down, and walls as well and water was pouring everywhere, just as my beautiful Christmas trees and decorations started turning on with their timers. I was in tears! All the hard work I had done to renovate - ruined! My biggest customer was calling nonstop but I could not talk to at the time. He ended up talking to the other businesses in town that I had sold to that week, and cancelled the now delivered orders. This meant I had to repay every penny and all shipping costs for each cancelled sale. That resulted in me losing my job.

My insurance company put myself, and a friend that was staying with me, up in a hotel for a week or so. This ended up being four solid months, with a dispute arising between the insurance company and the restoration company. The restoration company hauled off all my furniture and belongings in the storage containers in front of my house, as the insurance company refused to pay them. So they dropped me! My house was completely gutted from top to bottom, not livable in any way shape or form. The hotel ended up kicking us out as my insurance was not paying for it anymore. My friend and I had a major blowout, she was one of my dearest friends and went our separate ways. My heart broke!

My daughter and I went to Italy and signed the papers. I have so much faith that through all of this, going on, was still go forward I need you in Italy! ...Oh, there had now been three of us staying in the hotel as my daughter's visa was up in Scotland. We were kicked out of the hotel and had no place to stay. A kind customer from my part-time job (I was a manager of a restaurant) let us stay in his apartment, but failed to mention that his lights, gas and water had been turned off. For a full month we stayed there, and showered and used the bathrooms at the local gym. And we ate at work. Everything in my life had been destroyed in a flash! Everything! And so many more trials and hardships/heartbreaks - I could fill up volumes of books!

My worldly possessions were reduced to two suitcases, and one carry-on full of legal and business documents. I also still had a dream and pure faith, and somehow the courage, and funds, to move forward that I still go to Italy!

As my life was falling apart, God was putting it together in Italy, Sabbioneta, Italy to be exact! This has been such a tremendous walk of faith in my life, it took every ounce of faith and courage to go forward! I have been scared, lonely tired, hurt, destroyed, heartbroken, betrayed, humiliated, broke, broken, hungry, homeless, and felt like I was worthless in every sense of the word. my self-worth plummeted... and my self-confidence was even lower. I felt like I was a complete zero and all the grit I had left was to take one more step to go forward!

Heartbreak after heartbreak, and miracle after miracle. I tearfully hugged my daughter and told her I loved her. Alex said, "**Go, Momma! I Love you and Believe in you. This is where the Lord needs you!**"

"**Sometimes Faith will make you look stupid, and then it starts to Rain! Noah**"

I AM JO WIEHLER, I AM ENOUGH!!!

I am the owner of La Belle Sabbioneta, in Sabbioneta, Italy, the 500-year-old Miracle-of a Home that the Lord brought to me. It is a previous old Jewish Synagogue. 500 years ago, this was a dedicated house of the Lord! And the Owner of the Incredible Global PowerBall Team!

Have the courage to follow your dream, no matter what the cost. Go forward, have Faith, close your eyes and breathe. If your dreams are worth it, it won't be easy! Go Forward!

I am living proof that dreams do come true, and that God is Real! For every heartbreak, there is an equal or greater reward! Every tear will become a victory! And remember, God can do exceedingly, abundantly things above all that you can think or ask. Just Believe!

Thank you for allowing me to use my voice and speak my Intuitive Truth!

All my love,
Jo Wiehler

JO WIEHLER

Jo Wiehler is a Visionary and Business Owner and the founder of La Belle Sabbioneta®, La Belle Sabbioneta & The PowerBall Women®, La Belle Swagger®/ La Belle Brand ® which is dedicated to helping professionals and individuals level up in life by accessing their inner intelligence, talents,creativity, health, and wellness,- spiritually, physically, mentally, financially- all areas of life through guided Retreats and Tours in a safe and loving environment.

Known for her self-actualization, with her Sales, Marketing, and Branding skills Jo's vision for the future-leading with love and kindness Jo teaches business in a different way to break free from old cycles of limitation, time-proven, and extremely different–but highly effective marketing techniques and proven results.

Northern Italy is now where Jo calls home and business with specialised retreats from painting to writing to food and much more! Bringing her unique skills together and event management to the forefront you are going to want to be on retreat at La Belle Sabbioneta!

You can check out all the details via www.LaBelleSabbioneta.com
Facebook: facebook.com/labellesabbioneta
Instagram: Instagram.com/jowiehlerlabelle

20

JO-ANNE BROWN

FROM TRAUMA TO HEALING

*W*hen I was a little girl, I was strong, fearless and felt almost invincible.

One of my earliest memories is of watching in horror as a feral cat prepared to attack my younger sister who was playing with its kittens. At the time, I felt intensely protective and angry that any being would try to hurt her. Fortunately, I didn't have to intervene, but in that moment, I was ready to do whatever it took to keep her safe.

I was robust, healthy and I loved to learn. It seems that I also had an early aptitude for teaching. We were neighbours with an Italian family who had not long immigrated to Sydney, Australia. As well as being friends with the two little boys in the family, I was also teaching their mother to speak English. I was just four years old at the time.

And then suddenly my life changed. My family and I moved to one of the more industrial suburbs in western Sydney. After we moved, I became aware that my parents' relationship wasn't happy. As an almost-five-year-old, I found this distressing. My mind immediately considered the worst possible case scenarios.

What would happen to my younger sister and me? Who would take care of us? Would Dad be leaving us? Would that mean Mum would have to work? I was terrified that we would no longer continue to live as a family unit.

My little five-year-old self was grappling with questions that were too big for me to understand. The little girl who had previously been fearless and invincible suddenly didn't know what to do.

At this time, the measles virus was in full force. My younger sister and I caught the measles and stayed at home for the required quarantine period.

I became sick and was very weak. My former little self, that healthy, confident and fearless little girl, wasn't feeling so confident now! My little immune system was compromised, I lost 7 pounds and my ribs were showing. I developed bronchitis and started having problems breathing. My nose was always blocked, and I would wake up with my eyes crusted together. I could only breathe through my mouth (this continued until I was at least 30 years old). Before long, I was diagnosed with childhood asthma and prescribed medication by the doctor.

Many years later, I was to learn that our new suburb had the highest incidence of childhood asthma in Australia. Much of that was attributed to the environmental emissions from local industry.

Life changed drastically for me from that time on.

At the tender age of five, I was in a state of trauma that had started with a thought, a realisation of the potential for everything to go terribly wrong. I sensed that the breakdown of my family was inevitable. It was just a matter of time before it happened.

I was hypervigilant, while I waited for the other shoe to drop.

The thoughts that circulated through my head then led to feelings and emotions that were literally suffocating, as they became embedded and inflamed within my lungs, in the form of asthma.

I was struggling to breathe. It felt like a struggle for survival. Taking one breath in, trying to make it count, not knowing how long it was going to last. Letting go of that breath, releasing it, but at the same time resisting releasing the breath because I didn't know how many more breaths I would have before everything fell apart in my life.

I no longer felt powerful and strong. I felt disempowered and weak. I lost my confidence in my abilities and how I "read" the world.

I wasn't able to play as enthusiastically as I previously had. If I became over-excited, I would start wheezing and would have to sit down and watch the other children play together while I missed out.

I became more sensitive to the external environment. The colder weather would set off my asthma. In the summer, my eyes were irritated by the chlorine in the swimming pool so, once again, I would have to stop swimming, sit down and watch my friends play and have fun while I had to stay quiet and calm, so my asthma wasn't triggered.

While I was trying to adjust to my new hypersensitive way of interacting with the world, I was continuing to watch for signs of my family falling apart. It was a perpetual concern for me as I silently anticipated the inevitable collapse of my family.

In addition to my sensitivity to air quality and pool chemicals, I also became more sensitive emotionally.

Starting school brought with it both positive and negative experiences. My love of learning was obvious and I excelled academically. At the same time, I was extremely sensitive to being called the "brain" of the class and what I wanted most was to blend in and be like all of the other children.

I particularly loved mathematics and science subjects. For me, they represented absolutes, something I could depend upon, something I knew would always remain the same. I knew that $5 + 5$ would always equal 10, and that was beyond reassuring for me. I knew what was right and wrong there; the rules didn't change. I knew where I stood with maths and science.

After I finished primary school, my family moved from Sydney to Lake Macquarie, just south of Newcastle. The high school I attended with my younger sister was located in an entirely magical location, on the edge of the lake.

During high school, I continued to love mathematics and science subjects. They continued to be reliable, providing me with a sense of stability and security.

One of my greatest stress relievers during those years was through my involvement in the local community brass band. I was able to blow out all my teenage frustrations through my cornet during band practice. The band community was another constant for me, in the face of the family tension at home that continued to brew just below the surface.

At the end of my high school years, my parents eventually separated. On one level I was relieved. But on another level, each of us was adjusting to what was to become our "new normal".

In my years after high school, I had many wonderful experiences. One of the highlights of my early adult years was attending a church college in the United States where I met many wonderful people with whom I am still friends today.

When I returned from the States, I studied engineering and worked in both industry and consulting as an environmental engineer. During my early years in engineering, I continued to suffer from both asthma and severe migraine headaches. I learned (through repeated experiences) that pharmaceutical solutions did not seem to work for me, so I sought out more natural health options. After finding a frequency-based modality that used an applied understanding of Traditional Chinese Medicine, I started healing from asthma and migraine headaches and began to regain my confidence.

As I saw myself healing in a way that I hadn't thought possible, I made the decision to train in bioresonance therapy, the frequency-based modality that had transformed my life. Doing this work allowed me to help others in a tangible way which gave me a great sense of satisfaction.

While working as a natural therapist, I came to a very important realisation. Some of my clients were healing completely from long-term health problems. Other clients, however, were temporarily having health improvements that only lasted for short periods of time. After that, many of their original symptoms would return.

I had to find out why this was happening. I started to recognise the importance of the body-mind-spirit connection and realised that, in order to create permanent healing shifts, the person seeking healing had to be invested in their own personal healing on three levels, not just on the physical level.

It was essential to create an energetic shift on a mental level, that occurs within the belief system and thought patterns. It was also essential to create a positive shift on a spiritual or relational level, which addresses imbalances in our personal relationships – with self, others and/or our Higher Power/Source.

This awareness transformed my life.

When I look back on my childhood, I see that I relied on the stability and security that the sciences provided me. I found absolute answers in these subjects while at school and I trusted them implicitly. As I became an adult, I continued to trust the sciences as absolute authorities.

However, I realised that I hadn't developed the opposite end of the spectrum in my life; my more intuitive capabilities. My gut feelings. If anything, I had shut them down, choosing to put my faith in what had proven to be constant for me at that time.

This led to me on a quest to learn about intuition in a way that I could be comfortable with. In a way that integrated with all of the other areas of my life.

In my search, I discovered renowned intuitive and author, Cyndi Dale, who is also a most gracious teacher and mentor. Cyndi's understanding of energy recognises the validity of both intuition and science, so her teachings have eased me into working intuitively as well.

Now, I help my clients by drawing on both intuitive wisdom and the more rational scientific approaches, knowledge and understanding. And I encourage my clients to seek healing on the physical, mental and spiritual levels, rather than just on the physical level, so their healing is profoundly deep and sustained.

In my work, I draw on so many aspects of my background, including my childhood experiences, my engineering background and my natural therapy (bioresonance) training.

Through my childhood experiences, I know personally what it is like to feel traumatised by circumstances outside of your own control.

I felt an endless stream of conflicting feelings and emotions as I watched my family fall apart slowly over thirteen years, starting around my fifth birthday. As each year went by, I wondered if this would be the year that everything would disintegrate; I both feared and agonised over the many potential outcomes from the family breakdown.

And I was one of the lucky ones! Neither of my parents were neglectful; they were both attentive to my needs.

According to the Adverse Childhood Experiences (ACE) Study, what I experienced as a child isn't technically classified as trauma, since I did not experience the divorce or separation of a parent while I was under the age of eighteen.

However, Bonnie Badenoch includes a definition of trauma in her book *The Heart of Trauma: Healing the Embodied Brain in the Context of Relationships* that my childhood experience resonates with, where trauma is:

"any experience of fear and/or pain that doesn't have the support it needs to be digested and integrated into the flow of our developing brains."

Essentially, my little five-year-old developing brain had trouble making sense of my childhood experience. And for some reason, I carried the weight of my fear and pain alone, without sharing it with others.

In retrospect, I believe I had this experience so I could see how trauma, stuck emotions and feelings trigger the immune system, making us increasingly susceptible to disease patterns.

As an adult, I have been able to re-frame my childhood experience in a healthy way, with the help of friends, alternative health professionals and energy healers. I have also gained a better understanding of who I am through various archetypical systems including Astrology, Numerology, Enneagrams, and more recently Human Design. These systems have both explained and validated my sensitivities and helped me to recognise how I can use my strengths more effectively as I help others to re-frame their own difficult experiences.

Through my engineering background, I also help my clients make energetic shifts. I frequently receive guidance where an engineering application or analogy is shared to provide additional insight. I am honoured to be a conduit in this way so the lives of my clients are improved through the messages I receive for them.

I am thrilled that my engineering background feeds into my intuitive work and provides insights for both me and my clients. It reaffirms my belief in the existence of an intuition-science spectrum where we can be both intuitive and scientific or rational at the same time!

My natural therapy background also feeds into my intuitive work.

During my early thirties, while I was studying engineering, I was able to come to a place of resolution around my asthma. As a child, I didn't fully understand what was happening to me energetically. I knew I was struggling for breath, but I really didn't understand why. At the time, I felt stressed by the family dynamics and was trying to survive from day to day.

Through my natural therapy training, I learned that when I was a child, my little five-year-old lungs were weighed down by grief. Traditional Chinese Medicine views the lungs as the bodily organ that stores unresolved grief and other associated emotions when those emotions aren't able to be processed in a healthy way.

I learned that, in those childhood years, my immune system had buckled under a combined toxic load from that grief (and the unexpressed emotions I held within), microbial overload and air pollution.

My physical body was able to release the weight of much of this accumulated load from the microbial overload and toxins. I learned to release the trauma and grief in a way that was healthy for me. What a relief that was!

On my healing journey, I also came to see that engineers and intuitives really aren't that different.

In his book, *Applied Minds: How Engineers Think*, Guruprasad Madhavan describes how engineers tap into several different "streams of knowledge" and transform enormous challenges into opportunities. He believes that engineers are able to do that through their ability to see structure where none is apparent.

In my relatively unusual position as both a former engineer and a currently practising intuitive, I believe that this ability is also an aspect of the highly sensitive person (HSP), the empath and the intuitive.

Those of us who are highly sensitive are often more aware of the invisible world than the visible world we live in. We pick up on subtleties that others don't see. We are the proverbial canaries in the goldmine; detecting dangers and threats before most other humans do.

I believe there is both the intuitive and the engineer within each one of us, that allows us to delve into those unseen structures that shape our lives, to seek both understanding and to heal the broken aspects of ourselves so we are whole again.

There are three valuable lessons I learned from my childhood experience:

1. Our most difficult life experiences can reveal our life purpose.

There are events in our lives that are pivotal and life-changing. They can seem almost fated. I believe that this particular time period in my life – from four to six years of age – was one of those pivotal experiences in my personal life story that has strongly impacted my life choices and decisions.

While this experience caused me great pain, it also led me to seek personal healing and to learn every possible lesson I could from it. I have learned how to care for myself in three fundamental ways; improving my physical health, learning to understand how my personal beliefs and thoughts affected my health, and also gaining clarity around my relationships with myself, my family and others and the Divine being that I call God.

2. When we fully accept ourselves, we give others permission to fully accept themselves.

Being a sensitive person is something I have learned to appreciate about myself. Trying to ignore my sensitivities or pretending that I am not that way just doesn't work! But when I am helping a person through a difficult time, my sensitivities come to the fore. Time and time again, people are drawn to work with me because of my sensitivities, not in spite of them.

3. As we work through our own healing process, we are able to support others in their healing.

Healing from my childhood experience has allowed me to reach others who are hurting and struggling. It is literally part of my job description that I help highly sensitive people to embrace their life purpose and harmonise their inner wisdom, intelligence and in-body connections. I am essentially helping others to heal in the way I was able to heal.

Each of us has had experiences that enable us to empathise with and reach out to others. Starting our own healing process virtually qualifies us to help others to heal. This gives our life meaning and also allows us to transform our life difficulties through a beautiful alchemical process into something life-giving and beautiful.

And now, I'd like to encourage you to take some time to re-visit some of those experiences in your life that have been challenging or traumatic. Look for the gems of wisdom that you have learned through the pain of these experiences. And see how, like me, your life purpose may have been revealed to you during those difficult times, allowing you to both heal and to help others through what you have learned!

JO-ANNE BROWN

Jo-Anne is an energy healer who lives in central Queensland with her husband and two border collies, Jessie and Cody.

In her work, Jo helps highly sensitive people to integrate find meaning in their profound emotional experiences as they transform their pain into wisdom. In this process, they are able to recognise and release disharmonious belief systems, stuck emotions, disease patterns and toxicity.

Jo sees science and intuition as being on a continuous spectrum rather than being distinctly separate and views her work as a bridge where the energetic and the logical are woven together. Because of this, her background in both environmental engineering and bioresonance therapy add a unique quality to her healing sessions.

Jo works with clients all over the world through online sessions that are available through her website https://www.joanneintuitive.com.

You can also connect with her on
Facebook at https://www.facebook.com/joanneintuitive/.

MEREDITH ROSE

FROSTY THE SNOWMAN'S WIFE

*M*y heart sank grotesquely towards the floor, as did my stomach, as they did often in those days, as I was spoken over the top of yet again at the Christmas party in 2016. Each interruption, each brushing aside of my opinion and input, each flippant disregard, chipped away at my spirit and caused me to shrink and disbelieve my worthiness even more. Solidifying and intensifying the already-rampant doubt that I had in myself.

I had become so accustomed to being spoken over and halted mid-sentiment, that I yet again attempted to convince myself I wasn't bothered. That it was okay that I was interrupted; that it was because what I had to say didn't matter. That everyone else's input was much more interesting and valuable than mine.

I wasn't willing to examine the sensation or cause of my invisibility because on some level I knew how laborious and gargantuan the effort would be to mend what needed mending. When one truly feels worthless, the leap towards personal recognition of worth feels like one measured by light years, and I had not the energy nor compunction to instigate such effort.

The extreme level of self-loathing I had become comfortable with stemmed from many an experience in my youth, coupled with crippling shyness and timidity that I had seemingly been born with.

It equated to 37 years of debilitating bowing, apologising, shame, comparison, and obsessive people-pleasing.

Little did I know, throughout those 37 years, that the anxiety I suffered from was a side-effect of being disconnected from my worth. That the OCD I experienced was a desperate and fledgling attempt to establish control. That the way I was being named gullible and delusional by the fearful ones close to me, was a misinterpretation and mislabelling of my open heart and powerful intuition. That my belief in everyone else's narrative but my own, was the treacherous cousin of my self-doubt.

Little did I know that those who were telling me I was helpless and in need of a thicker skin, were the ones from whom I should not have been taking advice. That with each casting aside of the truth of who I was, the force of passion within me was incrementally stolen. And little did I know, that the disconnection from the one creative outlet that had made me feel joyful and special when I was a small girl was because of this, and not because my talent and love for it had dwindled.

That outlet was singing, and I adored it; not only for the sensation of divinity seemingly being channelled through me and the way it helped me experience love itself, but for how it seemed to please the adults.

However, as life took over, I encountered events and circumstances that would slowly crush my spirit one-by-one. The desire to sing simply funnelled away from me, so gradually that I didn't even notice it happening.

In primary school, the shyness in me seemed to satisfy and somehow fuel the bullies and their mission to humiliate and torture me. I was attacked about anything that stood out about me; specifically, the colour of my hair. 'Ghostie', 'Nanna', and 'Frosty the Snowman's Wife' don't seem like names that would cause any real psychological damage, but the vicious intent behind the taunts and the relentlessness of their delivery certainly were. I don't think I'll ever forget the time that the most popular girl in school spent weeks intricately tricking me into thinking we were best friends, only to orchestrate a grand display of public humiliation in the busy playground by revealing loudly, in a performance-style scene, that it had all been a joke.

Every night throughout those years I would squeeze my hands tight in prayer as I lay in bed, desperately praying that God would give me reprieve from their taunts the next day.

Perhaps this is where I began my incessant tendency to compare myself to others. I would study wistfully the qualities of the popular, loved students. They always seemed to have so much I didn't have. I became obsessed with studying the blatant and glaring gap between where they were and where I considered myself to be. My subconscious would become addicted to the insidiousness of comparison.

The bullying continued on into high school, where they had new things to tease me about, and I believed more and more that I was useless, untalented, ugly, and dorky.

A desperate yearning for acceptance and validation was a constant in my life, and I began to believe that if I said 'yes' to anything and everything asked of me and more, perhaps I would find that acceptance.

It was toward the end of high school that I wondered if I would be more liked if only I were thinner. I decided I would only eat a single raw carrot for lunch every day, no breakfast, and perhaps a forkful or two of dinner. I recall not wanting to brush my teeth for fear of the calories in the toothpaste.

It was a few months later that I discovered I could make myself vomit, which was wonderful in my self-loathing eyes, as it meant I could enjoy the action of eating again.

The hatred I felt for my body spread rapidly into the realm of my looks. When I looked in the mirror, all I could see was extreme ugliness. I repulsed myself. Over the years, it became difficult to even look.

I began cutting my skin with a pocketknife, feeling like I deserved the pain. Perhaps enjoying the way that people seemed to be concerned about me when they saw the evidence. It was one step closer to the acceptance I craved.

The eating disorders, self-harm, and discovery of mild drugs and alcohol meant that my previously excellent grades had diminished by high school graduation. I was able to add 'dumb' to the long list of qualities to hate about myself.

But still, I did as I was told, which at the time was to choose a career ("but don't aim too high, or you'll set yourself up for failure") and finding a mediocre job for life ("minimum wage is good enough for you"). So, on I trudged, awkwardly attempting to find myself. I stumbled through whatever I was told would be good for me by those who were not living in a way I admired, always being conditioned with the "you don't know what's best for you" story.

A few years after high school, I met the man who would become my husband and father of my children. Once married, something in me told me it would be easier to relax into a small, meek and inferior version of myself; inferior to the powerful and confident man beside me who would now provide for us, make decisions for us, and speak for us. Easier than doing the work that part of me knew needed doing, to heal from my traumas such that I could begin to fulfil my potential.

Perhaps it was my personal experience of patriarchy throughout my upbringing; all the times my grandmother had scolded me for letting my brother do the washing up when "that is the girls' job." Perhaps it was the overall conditioning of society-prescribed gender roles that were so prolific for this 80's baby. But despite my mother's best attempts to instil power in my sisters and I (her favourite t-shirt to dress me in read, "Anything boys can do, girls can do better" in big bold letters), somehow I still let my personal power tumble into my husband's hands. I became a willing participant in the relinquishment of my truth and voice.

I remained obedient, small in spirit and disempowered throughout my twin boys' pregnancy, and their birth in 2009 was fraught with intervention. The people-pleasing tendency demanded I say 'yes' when asked post-birth whether I was happy with the outcome, but I was simply unable to do so wholeheartedly, for I had hoped for more.

I experienced a similar story to many new mothers and became incredibly lost in a world of sleeplessness and identity confusion.

The Universe had a plan for me, though, and my spirit would soon get an injection of energy.

When my boys turned one, a book on Kundalini Yoga fell in my lap. It was the start of something powerful. However, whilst the practices were certainly beneficial, and launched me to new places of generous lifeforce and belly fire, the missing piece was always self-love.

Without self-love, I didn't honour this new passion of mine. I didn't prioritise my practice when it became logistically difficult. I didn't believe I was worthy of it. I let motherhood, and a clash in personalities between my husband and me, prevent me from pursuing the first potent passion I had ever found since I had given up singing.

However, this was not to be the end of my story.

It was when I experienced the drug-free, unassisted water birth of my daughter in 2017 that I finally began to open my eyes to the dynamic and infinite force I was; as all women are. Labouring and birthing in rhythm with how nature intended, broke me open in ways I hadn't expected. My mind began to expand from that point forward. Having a girl was also an integral piece to my journey towards self-love, as I would spend hours staring at her with all the exquisite love of a mother for her child, and would visualise her speaking to herself as I had been speaking to myself all these years. The very thought broke my heart into a million pieces, and I began to tentatively turn that compassion toward myself.

It was in these early months of my daughter's life that the term 'Highly Sensitive Person' (HSP) made its way into my awareness. Turns out that it is a studied and proven biological fact that there are those with an increased central nervous system, more sensitive to physical, emotional, and social stimuli.

Something in me clicked in a most glorious way when I learned that I wasn't broken, as many had suggested.

When I learned that I did not have to just grow a thick skin, as had been recommended to me by many people close to me.

When I learned that the intensity with which I felt emotion was not a flaw in my design, as I had begun to believe.

This new discovery led me to examine and understand why it had been my tendency to shrink when someone more abrasive and certain than I, took the reins of a situation. And why many events in my life had made such lasting and detrimental impact on my belief system.

The tendency in me to vilify the corresponding personal qualities began to flip, and I saw those qualities in a new light.

I began seeing them as my superpowers.

I began to develop an awareness of my awareness.

I began to observe myself with curiosity instead of hatred.

With this new understanding and recognition of subtleties, I began to realise that intuition did indeed exist.

All of a sudden, the countless memories of being told I was gullible, delusional and weak came flooding back, and an indignancy was born.

This new and surprising indignancy felt somehow preferable to mediocrity and powerlessness.

It had energy behind it, determination behind it, the spark of injustice fuelling a new conviction, a whisper to listen to. This suggested to me that perhaps I had been wrong to listen to the voices of contempt, disregard, and doubt in my abilities. That perhaps my former meekness had allowed others to walk all over me and be vampirical of my giving, loving energy.

All of a sudden, I had a new skill of being able to say "no". Using this word brought me mixed feelings. The not-enough-ness tried creeping in, but ultimately the honouring of my energy and my real desires felt GOOD.

A shocking, life-changing thing would then happen to me, shortly thereafter.

My husband announced his decision to depart from our relationship, without explanation.

You can imagine how terrifying and earth-shattering it was, to be facing single-motherhood, the keeping of a home and maintenance of an acreage, the creation of an income, and the finding of my elusive joy, after 15 years of letting my husband fill the gap that my powerlessness had created.

The man that I had believed I would be with forever, that I had put all my trust in and who had been my voice all this time, was ripped from me in a single moment.

The fear. The pain. The confusion. The panic.

I found myself in a wild place; territory completely unknown to me; odds seemingly against me for the rising above that needed to take place, lest I succumb to victimisation.

I knew I needed to let myself feel this with every inch of my heart, body and soul.

Immediately the habit I had so carefully instilled in myself to tongue-bite and squash my own spirit, caused that now-familiar indignancy to soar through my being.

Suddenly excruciating injustice and sheer fed-up-ness took me over, and I made a pact that I WOULD RISE.

I would not become a victim; I'd wasted far too many years doing that.

I would not let myself go backwards; I'd had glimpses of my potential and I knew I was strong.

Most importantly, I would not politely submit to the parasitic voice that had been placed in me that told me I needed looking after; that I knew not what I needed; that I was inferior and helpless.

My recent lesson in acknowledging my intuition began to serve me. For my intuition told me I needed to find a way to love myself. Wholly. Unapologetically. Fiercely.

My intuition told me that first I needed to grieve; to mourn the lost years and the wasted opportunities to love myself and live with fervour.

It took months. I let it be wild and cathartic; it was messy, it was non-linear, it was beautiful.

In those months, I began forcing myself to look in the mirror. As laborious as it was, as much as my trauma-fuelled habits were screaming at me to look away, I would force my eyes from feature to feature. I wouldn't let my eyes come away from each resting place until I had found a narrative deep within me, one of appreciation and love. I began looking deep into my own eyes and forcing a phrase over and past my dry tongue and lips.

"I love you."

Over and over again.

At first, disbelieving it. Impossible to receive the notion. Yet knowing I could not allow myself to ease that practice until I started feeling the words in my cells, and believing them.

My self-love and spirit started coming back in small increments.

And I began to sing again.

These glimpses I'd had into trusting my intuition were exhilarating to me. So when the concept of personal branding and a means for creating abundance I'd never believed I was capable of, made itself known to me, I wanted to play.

The old story said I couldn't do it.

But the new story I wanted to write said, "Goshdarn, I want to see."

The new story I wanted to write said I would provide in big, beautiful, powerful ways for my babies, and I would singlehandedly give them an amazing life. The new story I wanted to write said I could fulfil my innate desire to help others by guiding them to acknowledge the things I had acknowledged in myself – their power, their uniqueness, their truth and their worth – through my own personal brand, and theirs.

The synchronicity of how personal branding is about unleashing one's voice, and the journey I'd been on to unleash my own, was not lost on me.

The gratitude and open-heartedness that shot through me in those wild times continued to fuel me as I got to work. My shakti continued rising as I experienced the medicine of personal branding and the way it demanded that I pursue my passions. The energy would spill out through words, song, and mantra. I was able to start taking the steps toward conquering my shyness and turning the sinister whisper of not-good-enough-ness around into one of unleashed spirit and creative flow.

The contrast between the 37 years of feeling crushed, and the lifetime I have before me of truth, sound, and power, takes me on a continually upward-moving spiral towards a higher and higher vibration, as I weave my magic into the online space, call in abundance to support me on my mission, and help and teach other beautiful women to do the same.

The lessons I learned on my journey brought crystalline clarity that the ways I had been subconsciously choosing disconnection from my truth were severely damaging.

My eyes opened.
My mind expanded.
My heart was broken open.
And my voice made its way out.

Now I can't remember the last time my heart sank grotesquely toward the floor.

And if someone were to call me "Frosty the Snowman's Wife" now, well, I don't believe I would blink an eye.

LESSONS LEARNED:

I see now, that the alternative of loving myself fiercely was the cause of total chaos in my world.

That obsessive people-pleasing was the means for perpetual disconnection from my worth and truth, and that saying no is an act of self-love.

That injustice mixed with belly fire can be a powerful catalyst for a healing journey.

Whilst being careful that the subsequent actions in response to the above realisations caused no harm to others, I launched myself to new places of worthiness and determination. There was no need, then, to dwell on any injustices or let them poison me.

So please, beautiful reader, know that you are worthy. Know that you are perfect as you are. Know that others' stories of doubt in your capability are not yours to carry. Know that to love yourself is the most important thing you can do, for the ripple effect you shall instigate has immense power to change the world.

It's never too late.

But don't waste another minute.

MEREDITH ROSE

As a Highly Sensitive Person who had grown up thinking she was broken, Meredith Rose once resided in realms of disempowerment, self-loathing, and mediocrity. With no knowledge of her potential, she played small and allowed her voice to be squashed.

Through a series of spontaneous events, Meredith was launched by the Universe into a healing journey that would see her not only recover completely from what was limiting and crushing her, but also learn to know, love, and trust her soul's purpose.

Meredith Rose is now passionate about guiding others to become the bright, abundant, powerful, truth-drenched person they were born to be, through the medicine that helped her on her journey and calling in abundance.

She is a single mother of three, a Kundalini and Hatha Yoga teacher, Sound Healer, Bhakti Musician, Reiki Practitioner, and conscious, heart-centred Personal Branding Coach.

Contact Meredith...
Website: www.meredithrose.com.au
Facebook: www.facebook.com/meredithrose1234
Instagram: www.instagram.com/theofficialmeredithrose

22

MADELEINE P WOBER

LIVING MAGICALLY

FROM THE BEGINNING:

I was born to speak! As a baby, sitting in my pram in Scotland, I'd say 'Hello man' to passers-by, and though it was decades ago, I remember this clearly. From the beginning, I thrived on connection and communication. An old soul, a free spirit. I could feel what people were feeling as though it was happening to me.

At age 2½, I was already experiencing living magically.

I parked my dolls in their pram, at the end of the street, and ventured into the swing park across the main road. I got chatting to a lady who offered me chocolate, (the best day of my life), and a huge burly policeman who brought me home to my poor, frantic mother, who had been out with the neighbours searching for me (the worst day of her life). I was free, curious, and tapped into unlimited possibilities. That open-hearted wanderer was my true nature, and my angels were protecting me.

I've always followed my heart. I knew I was different. I believed that I was an earth angel, put here to help people. This meant rushing to the rescue in the playground if witnessing a kid being bullied, or marching fearlessly up to older boys in the midst of a huge fight.

My mother kept a close watch over me after the swing park incident. Feeling stifled and controlled, I was happiest when watching American TV shows on a Saturday morning (Charlie's Angels, Fantasy Island, Magnum PI, Kids From Fame). During the rainy days, I declared that someday I'd be living in America. I loved daydreaming about driving around in my shiny red sports car, like Magnum PI.

My youthful opinion wasn't respected, and was met with 'we say black you say white'. I wasn't allowed to wear what I wanted, have my hair the way I liked, and my truth was often taken the wrong way. By the time I was a teenager, I felt incredibly controlled and trapped, longing to leave, and see the world. Although I attended a highly academic school, I wasn't the academic type. My EQ was always way higher than my IQ, but I passed the important exams at school, with minimum effort. My dream then was to become an actress in New York, however, I had to navigate life's challenges and myself, to get there.

I discovered that writing poetry, specifically outdoors, was an outlet for me to express myself, especially when I was in a dark place. I learned that each creature that scurried across my path or crawled upon my hand, had a message for me.

TAKING FLIGHT:

At 18, a serendipitous opportunity presented itself for me to go and live in California, and au pair, for three young girls. I felt like I was Maria from the Sound of Music, with a huge responsibility, and being so young, it was both terrifying and thrilling. On day one, their mother left on a business trip, and the youngest ran away. Karma! I was being shown how my mother, (just three years older than I was at the time), must have felt when I had done the same thing!

These beautiful, mischievous young girls grew up, married, eventually had children of their own, and today 30 years later, we are all great friends. I still adore their mum who I nicknamed my Fairy Godmother. California was 'home' for me, and provided times of great joy, but I chose to return back to the UK to attend university in Manchester, England to study Retail Marketing and Business. I followed many of my friends there because I didn't want to miss out, but after the California experience, I was so miserable, and life was peppered with intense anxiety. I was living by the mantra "Fake it 'till you make it". Every morning, I'd drag myself out of bed, put a smile on my face, and hit automatic pilot. Even though all I wanted to do was disappear, this lie I was living got me voted as the class rep, known for my positive attitude and helpful nature. A couple of years in, I couldn't take it anymore and quit abruptly. I had been romantically involved with a Mancunian guy called Jim, and although I tried, we never said goodbye.

FALLING APART & FALLING INTO PLACE:

I moved to London to study Beauty Therapy in the London College of Fashion in my mid 20's and while it was more creative, I developed chronic anxiety, severe depression, ongoing paralyzing panic attacks, and suicidal thoughts. This was who I had become, and at the time I couldn't see past each day.

For two years, I had to rewire my mind to think rationally, when light, and positivity seemed unobtainable. Eventually, with professional help, I managed to conquer this overwhelming terrain.

That summer, I travelled around Europe, always happiest and most comfortable when on the road, meeting people, exploring and photographing stunning sites, and allowing the flow of serendipity back into my life where every day felt magical! Intuition always kept me on point even when it defied logic. When I listened to my heart, things fell into place. When I tried to force things, it made me unhappy.

When I tap into living magically, the mundane is transformed into miracles. The insurmountable obstacles become resilient revelations, and I am stronger than I think. There is a deep inner confidence that emerges. There is no longer any need to 'fake it 'til you make it'.

After my student years, I knew I wanted to travel more, and still had dreams on my bucket list, so 3 years later, I backpacked around the world with my younger sister, and once again fell into the flow state of ease, and living magically. I was in love with life, and the more I ventured, the freer I felt. Things happened effortlessly because I was present and open: jobs, relationships, accommodation, and friendships. It was all unfolding naturally and had very little to do with me trying to make it happen. I didn't always know initially why I was led to specific people, places or things, but the answer always revealed itself. I had various past life regression sessions after continuous serendipitous events, that made me question if I had met these people before. World travel led me to connect more deeply with the Angels and what I wanted to do next! Attend acting school in New York.

Life is a roller-coaster, and weaved in amongst all the magic, there is always something momentous to learn. 'As you get better, the game gets bigger' (Andrew Matthews). With each stride forward, the greater my next obstacle. Each decade since my 20's, huge challenges have been presented to me. In my 30's, at the point I was ready to start meeting with agents, my acting career was interrupted after finding out I had Ovarian Cancer, and then, in my mid 40's, once I had finally reached my pinnacle position of legally landing a job in California, I was diagnosed with Multiple Sclerosis. What was this journey of health issues trying to show me, and how could I find the silver linings in all of this? I knew there were things I still had to heal, and learn lessons, including unapologetically speaking my truth.

SERENDIPITIES:

There have been many encounters with Angels, which have always guided me. For example, they helped me in 2018, in Scotland, while trying to find my Grandma's grave in the huge Jewish cemetery. I had been walking around for 15 minutes with no clue where to find her, then I heard this voice guiding me, step by step, with very specific instructions, until eventually, it said "look down", and there at my feet was my Grandma's grave, right next to my Grandpa. It was a precious and sacred moment. It was a phenomenal reminder that day, that if I quiet my ego and listen, I can fully trust that guiding voice.

My dream of settling in the US manifested, and it came time to buy a car in California. After test driving a series of black Jeeps, my dream shiny red sports car revealed itself in the form of a fabulous VW Bug. It wasn't there when I first arrived, but seconds before I was about to sign a contract for a car way above my means, I looked out into the parking lot of the car dealership, and there she was! She was the perfect car for me and in my price range. I signed on the dotted line and drove away in my shiny red sports car.

A year later, a lady with a puppy under her arm, was leaving the gym at the exact moment I was arriving. That whole week I had been talking about how much I wanted a dog, and this lady desperately needed to find a home for her puppy. We exchanged numbers, and 2 weeks later, Jasmine was mine.

I met my fiancé in California. We worked in the same office for 18 months but had never properly spoken. We had both become newly single at the same time, and one late evening at the office, it was like a romantic rendezvous from a classic movie. Clearly, we were meant to cross paths. When the timing is right and the stars are aligned, you just know it.

I would bump into people from the UK, from my past, in seemingly random locations. I was coming out of the subway at Union Square in New York, it was dark and pouring with rain. Hood over my head, eyes on the ground watching where my feet were walking, I could hear a guy talking in front of me with an extremely familiar voice, a Mancunian accent. I quickened my pace to try catching up with him. and the lady he was walking with. We all stopped waiting for the lights to change so we could continue crossing the road and, to my disbelief, I saw it was Jim! The old flame from Manchester who I had tried to connect with before I abruptly left the course. We had a lovely conversation, both of us in shock that this was actually happening 10 years later. It made me tune in to the incredible concept of divine timing

I could continue with many more mind-blowing stories. Perhaps in another book!

When these things happen, in a split second, it's a sliding doors moment, and it makes me think of all the things that had to happen for us to cross paths at that exact second.

So much magic. I feel super excited right now sharing these events with you.

So why am I sharing this with you!?

Serendipities are the angels winking at you. When they happen, get excited!

Remember you are unique. There is only one of you in the world. This is a miracle. We are so much more than the stories we tell ourselves, about who we think we are. March to the beat of your own drum, and live a truly magical and passionate life.

LIFE LESSONS:

As a child, I frequently got shamed and scolded for speaking, and was once firmly asked to pick up my desk and move out into the corridor. Years later I would go into radio and become a talk show host with numerous programs.

Yes very often, the very thing we were criticized for in our childhood is in fact our superpower.

Speaking became a huge part of my success. Over the years, building rapport with clients in the corporate world allowed me to gain their trust and win highly lucrative projects. Later I was lead to Transformational Empowerment Coaching, and now, I combine that skill with Spirituality and the Angelic Realm.

It took me many years to have the courage to speak my truth, share my opinion, and unashamedly express my enthusiasm for life. My positivity was often taken for sarcasm and met with resistance and skepticism from work colleagues, but it was something I treasured.

My tagline is 'Delivering Sage Wisdom with Childlike Enthusiasm'

I know I'm here to make others feel good about themselves, to empower, and to give hope. I can only speak from my own experiences: countless challenges, and many inexplicable, incredibly magical moments. MY GREATEST LIFE LESSON, SPEAKING MY TRUTH, IS THE MOST IMPORTANT THING I CAN DO – FOR MYSELF AND FOR OTHERS. Another quote: "Those who mind don't matter and those who matter don't mind" (Bernard Baruch)

Here are some of my greatest truths:

Music is my muse.

There is no such thing as coincidence.

A nomad at heart, I'm happiest when my life takes me to new places.

The meaning of life is an ongoing project.

I don't belong anywhere & I belong everywhere.

Some of my decisions look impulsive, but to me, they are calculated risks.

I belong to no one and in my relationship, I choose to be 100% monogamous.

I love living alone. My ideal would be to live next door to my life partner. Maybe with a secret door between the two dwellings.

I'm a master manifestor and whatever I dream of comes to me.

It feels great to own my eccentric side.

I love my childlike enthusiasm.

I love talking to strangers, many have become close friends (or lovers).

I am terrified of heights and big spiders.

My intuition guides me, catapults me, saves me and excites me. It is always right.

I'm a night owl and do my best work between midnight and 3 am.

I can be the life and soul of the party, but I'm not a party animal.

I'm an extroverted introvert. I love my space. I love to meditate and need time alone.

I receive my greatest creative bursts and ideas from being in nature and/or when I'm on a plane or driving somewhere.

I'm proud to be an Aquarian with all my quirks.

No matter how horrible another human's behaviour is, I can always look for the good in them and empathize with their pain.

I have learned to see the most challenging people as my greatest teachers.

My top values in life are the 4 C's: Connection, Communication, Compassion, Creative Collaboration. Everything I teach/share today is based on these values.

As spiritual beings having a human experience on earth: the depth, the struggles, the highs and lows, the feeling lost, and then following the signs, finding our truth, is what we all signed up for before we got here.

As I approach 50, I speak my truth in every relationship, this is non-negotiable. I aim to communicate with love, remembering to see the other as a soul, not a role.

Being a strong connector, throughout the years I landed in sales jobs bringing in millions for the companies I worked for. I would rise to the top effortlessly and I realized that the reason I was in that job, surrounded by these people, at that time, was purely to learn about myself, or to teach something, often to top management or owners.

In February 2020, I received a message from my Guardian Angel, to help people worldwide, to combine my Transformational Empowerment Coaching with Spirituality, and connect them to the Angelic realm. I listened to this guidance. I'm in awe of the messages that unfold for my clients, and the epiphanies they leave with. When I'm speaking, I often feel the words coming through me, not from me. I am so grateful that technology allows me to reach people everywhere. An unforeseen blessing during the Pandemic. Silver linings!

I can count 5 reasons on my right hand why my life is the best it's ever been and, at the same time count on my left hand, 5 reasons why my life sucks. Which hand do I want to focus on? Both can be my truth.

My truth is the reality I choose for myself. It's all frame of mind. It's about awareness and mindfulness. Using powerful spiritual practices, such as prayer, meditation and chanting, allows me to remember that although these take a lifetime, and are never fully mastered if I practice anyway, it will continually give me light and hope. 'A little bit of light dispels a lot of darkness' (Rabbi Schneur Zalman of Liadi).

When times get really dark, the magic of life is still all around us. We often don't see it, might not feel it, but it's there. Sure as the sun rises and sets every day, loving you, and shining on you unconditionally. Life is full of 2nd chances, take what you have learned, keep looking for the magnificent abundance, and heartbreakingly beautiful miracles in life, and never give up hope!

Every moment, I have the power, and choice, to shine my light and live a truly magical life, and guess what ...so do you!

My top 4 tips on Living Magically and Truthfully.

1. Be Authentic- know not everyone will agree with you or even like what you say, but say it anyway and always with a kind heart. You can't change others, only yourself, so don't expect anything, and if they hear /agree with you, that's a bonus.
2. Remain unattached to the outcome – Dream until your heart is full. Visualize, and take action, and then let it go. Have faith that it's not a case of IF it will happen, it's WHEN, which may not be on your timeline.
3. Own it - know your life experiences are unique to you, and that no one has walked in your shoes. Trust your discernment, your values, and the things you love about yourself, despite the opinions of others. Share your gifts and truths with the world.
4. Less Is More - sometimes your power is in your silence, and not in trying so hard to be heard. You matter. The world is richer because YOU are in it!

MADELEINE P WOBER

Madeleine P Wober (aka Maddie Sparkles, America's Scottish Sparkle) delivers Sage Wisdom with Childlike Enthusiasm, connecting people to their Internal Light & Guardian Angels. After three decades of medical setbacks including severe anxiety, depression, panic attacks and suicidal thoughts in her 20's, ovarian cancer in her 30's and diagnosed with MS in her 40's, she now helps others release their fears, step into their power, and find the silver linings, so they live a truly magical life by feeling divinely guided.

Maddie Sparkles, Intuitive Healer (working with the angels & spirit guides), Voice Actor, Inspirational Poet & Transformational Empowerment Coach, illuminates the path of Living Magically. She runs Living Magically retreats globally, has a vibrant Facebook community and offers Angel & Oracle card readings for healing in any area of your life.

To book your spot on the Living Magically Retreat in Italy (Summer 2022):
www.wetravel.com/trips/la-belle-sabbioneta-welcomes-maddie-sparkles-la-belle-sabbioneta-b-b-la-belle-brand-sabbioneta-48345565

Website: www.maddiesparkles.com
Facebook: www.facebook.com/groups/2535242876563100/
Instagram: www.instagram.com/maddie_sparkles_8

23

TARA ALLIE HARDAGE

SOFT SOUL, MEDIUM OPPORTUNITIES, & HARD CHOICES

*H*onestly, it was a complete accident rediscovering my spiritual gifts and becoming a psychic medium. Yet, once the door to this world was open again, things could never return to the way they were. As an active duty Sailor for over ten years, I assumed answering the call to service was my life purpose. However, at this time, new and conflicting energies were nudging my life to take a different path. Although I could feel this shift intuitively, I was not fully conscious of what would manifest if I proceeded into this unfamiliar territory. For as long as I could, I ignored it; the funny thing about the spirit, though, is it refuses to be ignored and will make itself known. Thus, it was a constant battle of my imagination running as free as a wild horse, and at the same time, having to rope it in with harsh words disguised as constructive-real world criticism. In the real world, people don't chase their dreams; they find employment, settle down, and slowly ease into often mundane routines of life. Dreaming was a luxury allotted to children, who are shielded from adult worries and responsibilities if allowed to take advantage of their childhoods. Technically, in my line of work, I had no business chasing my inner child and spirit's passions; there was work to be done. As an E-6 electrician in the Navy, engineering was no playground, especially for females, where Sailors must approach every task assigned pragmatically. In the military, intuition, imagination, and feelings are of little use for understandable reasons, which I found increasingly difficult to identify with as time went on. My mind knew that being realistic and empirical was vital to my continued success in the military. However, there was no getting around it; in my heart, if it was spiritual, I gravitated towards it. It did not matter the culture, the origin; if it felt good and uplifting, or mysterious and unexplained, I was all about it. In fact, after completing my military responsibilities and duties, one could often find me in the depths of all things unexplained, mystical, and spiritual. I, the moth, and the mysterious invisible universe that I could not objectively see but felt was all around me, was surely the flame. If I am truthful with myself, it was a flame I desired to consume me. Although the engineering world did not have a fraction of the appeal of the spirit world, it did not stop me from giving my very best effort. I received awards as prestigious as the Navy Achievement Medal three times. I also won Sailor of the Year, the fiscal year 2016-2017 aboard the U.S.S. Ronald Reagan CVN 76, an aircraft carrier home and work environment to a couple of thousand Sailors and D.O.D. counterparts. I achieved the rank of E-6 in roughly five years, which is a feat in itself. Additionally, my efforts and leadership led junior Sailors to complete countless electrical repairs, vital training, and numerous recognitions. I was honored to be a part of the mission and truly grateful for the opportunities it helped me offer to others and myself. But if I was honest with myself, even these prestigious accolades never quite filled the "hole." Additionally, at this time, what had originally started as a gentle nudge from spirit, was starting to feel like a firm pull. This concept puzzled me; I had success, rank, and purpose but could not shake the feeling that I had not yet even begun to pursue my true purpose. I continued to tell myself, "why do you want to throw all of your hard work away on something you are not quite sure you would be successful in ?" The logical side often argued inevitable failure due to a lack of physical evidence of this new path's success. In other words, "I had been successful in the Navy. Why did I want to risk it on something I was not even sure was my career calling ?" At this time, my plate was nearly full; the Navy was a big portion of that. Coming in a close second was college at Grand Canyon University. I was pursuing a degree in psychology. My original degree plan was business because it was marketable, and most importantly, it was acceptable. However, I changed it based on the logic that if I planned to reach 20 years in the Navy and retire, I would most likely not be using it solely to score a career. This theory convinced me that it was okay to study a field that was more intriguing to me. I enjoyed college very much, for the first time, I was asked to write, debate, and research more abstract topics such as human behavior, social influences, and the chemical make-up of the brain, to name a few. Although I was overjoyed to be exploring the field of psychology, there were roadblocks to my intuitive and spiritual beliefs. Even the field of psychology heavily relies on a term referred to as empirical evidence. It refers to only verifiable evidence that can be analyzed, observed, and collected. Although I believe 99% of the time, this method is superior for acquiring data for scientific purposes. I found myself to be in the one percent. The one percent are people who believe in science yet equally believe in spiritual theories and concepts that, if approached empirically, would be quickly dismissed. For instance, scientifically, how could one explain perceiving and hearing spirits, energy shifts, and psychic dreams. Surely, if approached from a scientific or medical perspective, one might assume the person to have Schizophrenia or psychosis. If labelled with these diagnoses, a person can go from believing they have a gift to believing they have a mental illness. Again, some people have mental illnesses, and medical solutions are necessary interventions. However, for those select individuals that do have a gift, it is vital to their journey they do not fail prey to the belief they are mentally broken, strange, or sick. When in fact, they are just the opposite intune, special, and gifted. I learned how special spiritual gifts were from a very young age. Although I would not consider my childhood to be perfect in any way, I have always considered myself very lucky that my mom was quite the intuitive herself and known for her accurate tarot card readings. Every time I told her what I saw, heard, or dreamed, she believed me and taught me how to speak with spirit to the best of her knowledge at the time. However, I watched my mom's passions and dreams as a psychic slowly fade as material-based needs and goals took the forefront throughout my upbringing. In her case, it had not ever paid the bills, but back in her days, she only accepted donations; she did not have today's social media outlets and technological resources. In her time, all clients that came were through word of mouth. So many people enjoyed my mother's readings; she loved to read so much often she would do it for free; when individuals expressed to her, they were low on funds. However, not everyone supported my mother's gifts, and those who disagreed attempted to make things hard for her. She faced religious, racial, gender ridicule. In the end, it was not people's opinions that won; it was financial stability that took the front seat, a justifiable reason for a mom of three. Many times she did what she had to, not exactly what she wanted to do. I was afraid that a similar outcome would happen to me. I watched my mom struggle internally and financially and promised myself that I would get the most stable job I could find when I was older. Something I was proud of, dependable, and that I felt I could make a difference through. However, I was 28 years old, with a college degree and a high-paying dependable job; I had achieved my goals, yet my spirit was urging me towards spiritual pursuits into the unknown.

A good amount of months passed, with these thoughts weighing heaving on my mind. Every waking moment, I was not actively engaged in electrical troubleshooting, homework, or sleeping; I was negotiating with the spirit world. I remember saying, "if this is really what you guys want me to do, I need a big sign, I need a teacher, I need something!" I was so frustrated! If a person asked their boss a question in the military, the individual got an answer, either a "yes or no," but there seemed to be silence as I begged the spirit world for my answers. Why did they have to be so mysterious, I thought? I immaturely remember saying, "fine! If I don't get an answer, I'll take that as an answer!" The funny part is deep down, the spirit world and I both knew something; I was not going anywhere. I compare it to being on the phone and being asked to wait on a very long hold; only someone who truly cares or is genuinely interested is willing to remain despite the urge to hang up. Let us just say the spirit realm had me on hold for a while now, and although I was frustrated, subconsciously, I knew I had no intention of hanging up.

Looking back now, I can not pinpoint the exact moment, but I remember receiving my answer. I was watching a documentary on psychics; it talked about how there were particular sites where psychics and mediums could join and practice in a safe, non-judgmental environment; it was then that something in my brain clicked. Public practising is what I need to do, I thought, this would help me decide. Undoubtedly, the next step would be to come to terms with my gifts. Were my abilities meant to share with close friends and family or the world as a full-time psychic medium? Simultaneously, I felt a rush of intense fear and excitement; if the latter turned out to be accurate, this would complete me on mind, body, and soul level, which is what I had subconsciously been searching after for quite some time. Yet another part of me has filled me with anxiety and doubt about starting over from nothing to chase such a rare and abstract calling. I knew practising on a public platform and gathering feedback from the departed loved ones, and verifying the information with the living ones was the first step to proving to myself this gift had global outreach.

I remember joining a few groups and not giving any practice readings for the first two months because I was afraid to be wrong. I was worried that one misinterpreted piece of evidence, along with a harsh "no none of that resonates" from the living, would crush me. In other words, it was a combination of all of these factors that made it so intimidating, in the beginning, for me to build the courage to give messages on a public platform.

However, after meditating and talking with my spirit guides, I'll never forget receiving the message to just do it! " I am not ready," I thought. Worse case scenarios would play in my head of statistically unlikely events. " What if nothing comes? What if the loved one gets angry with me? What if I misinterpret something from spirit?" All of the what-ifs were filling me with doubt. I told myself I was just going to check in on one of the psychic groups and scroll, no pressure. Only if I felt the spirit undeniably strong, I would write two things. At this point, I had seen pictures that I felt an intuitive pull to, but I always found a reason not to put out my evidence publicly. As I was was scrolling, I found a picture of a young man. I heard a gunshot, and I saw lots of trees. Nervously, I wrote, "I feel this young man had a tragic passing involving a gun, and I feel he passed in a wooded area." There were no other comments, so I waited for what felt like an eternity for the loved one to reply. The following day, I was shocked to learn that what I had seen, vividly depicted what happened. I continued contact with the young man in spirit, and extraordinary evidence came through. Honestly, I was in more shock than the loved one because this was my first time seeing spirit in action, and when spirit is truly in action, the accuracy is unbelievable. However, this healing confirmation was short-lived because I started to doubt. I thought, "what if that was just a series of lucky guesses?" The thought of this brought me back to reality. I knew to combat this next part of doubt, I would have to have statistical evidence, proving the odds were more than mere luck. As a result, I started doing as many free readings as I could connect to; I had to know if I was lucky or if this was a gift.

However, the visions and the feeling stayed consistent. My confidence was quickly soaring! Anyone that has the gift of psychic mediumship will explain it's a feeling like no other. Providing spiritual readings is both humbling and empowering at the same time. An old saying about soul mates is that when a person finds their soulmate, the person will just know, well, the same goes for an individual's soul purpose. I believe the moment the person starts working towards it, it will be unlike anything that person has ever done in their life. Of course, there will be challenges and roadblocks, but it won't matter because nothing can stand in the way of a person and their purpose; nothing but the person. In other words, I no longer thought this was my purpose; I knew this was my purpose! Admittedly, I wanted to stand for everything mediumship represented. Mediumship and spirit communication is everything in a calling I had ever wanted. Service to humankind, evidence, mystery, healing, spiritual empowerment, etc. For a healing soul such as myself, it was an understatement to say I was in heaven. However, for humans, Heaven must be grounded with earth, a lesson I was to learn.

Many would assume that such a triumphant discovery of my true purpose is the end of the story. However, to say that after discovering my gifts' potential reach, everything was perfect, would be a complete lie. Spirit world allowed me to experience a glimpse of my abilities, and it was up to me to put in the hard work. It is much like being gifted a vehicle; a gift does not mean it is free of maintenance, time, and care. In the beginning, this concept never crossed my mind. I was so obsessed with my new purpose I did not notice the balance of my life shifting to orbit only around readings and all things spiritual. As a disciplined personality, I had never struggled with motivating myself, setting goals, and progressing quickly. As a result, I treated my new spiritual endeavor as I would anything else in my life with a "go-getter mentality." I constructed timelines, goals, and objectives. After a few months of me staying up late and waking up early to practice, read, and immerse myself further into this world than before, I realized that the ambitious efforts that had worked so well for me in school and the military were not getting me anywhere. I had made my first big mistake, which is common of most lightworkers, by assuming that the spiritual world works on the timetable people layout; in reality, it is quite the opposite. Confidently, I monologued to the spirit world about how I wanted to continue to grow my gifts until they were as polished as the most remarkable mediums in history. Yet all my practice was not progressing me to the enormously high standards I placed on myself.

During this period, an older man in spirit, who resembled Santa Clause, with a shorter beard, and a few others, appeared for guidance. They explained that I would have to work hard to advance to the next level. I remember looking confused at the group of spirits appearing in my mind's eye. I had been overworking myself for months, what did they mean, work hard? They explained that my gift is one of interconnection, meaning it takes mind, body, and spirit to reach the peaks to which I aspire, as the greats had done before me. I would need to modify my diet and exercise to standards balanced for my body. I would need to read and learn to expand my mind, especially outside my comfort zone. I would need to address my anxiety and depressive symptoms that would often pop up but I would ignore. Lastly, I would have to come to terms with the concept that everyone's spirit is a perfect reflection of Source, God, or the Universe. However, there was no such thing as being perfect in this three-dimensional reality, especially the perfect person. I would have to accept that mistakes, challenges, and disappointments were inevitable in this human journey. My guides explained that I had chosen to be here. However, going down the path of purpose did not mean easy and simple. Instead, it meant it was worth the difficulties that arose. These are the lessons that changed me the most, not solely the rediscovery of my gifts but working on being the best human being that was feasibly possible for my standards, and not the world's standards.

I remind myself often that a flower will flourish under the right conditions; faith, confidence, love, and consistency. The same goes for those who, like the flower, also have a beautiful gift to display. Faith that one's passions will lead them on the path destined for them. Confidence in one's abilities to handle the advantages and challenges that may arise. Love for oneself and others. Being consistent in working towards bettering oneself on a physical, mental, emotional, and spiritual level, in whatever way, resonates with the person's values, morals, and lifestyles. Most importantly, remembering love is the true key to progressing, and the more love, the further one will go. It takes love to unfold one's gifts and love to be patient enough to watch this miraculous journey called life as it takes shape.

TARA ALLIE HARDAGE

Tara Allie Hardage is a Certified Reiki Healer, Spiritual Coach, and gifted Psychic Medium. Tara discovered her spiritual abilities to hear, see, and feel Spirit at the age of four; it was then that she began speaking with passed loved ones and guides, and then relayed these intuitive messages and dreams to her family. They supported her gift and Tara was particularly encouraged to develop further by her mother, a well-known intuitive specializing in tarot and energy reading.

Tara has delivered thousands of psychic and mediumistic messages, healings, and spiritual advice to individuals worldwide, providing her clients closure, support, and guidance. Her discipline and dedication are unmatched, which often she accredits to her prior military service to her country for helping to cultivate. Tara graduated her bachelor's in Psychology from Grand Canyon University with honors. She utilizes her psychological background to professionally and effectively address her clients' spiritual and emotional needs, providing spiritual and practical guides.

Website: www.tarathemedium.com/
Tiktok : TaraTheMedium
Instagram: TaratheMedium

24

LINDA EMSLIE

THE ART OF DISCERNMENT

Discernment is accessing the wisdom of our intuition to discover what is essential and true. Detaching from our desire to rush decisions, we seek to distinguish the true from the false, the facts from our assumptions and then choose the best path. Reflecting in silence creates space for our deepest perceptions. With contemplative vigilance, we open ourselves to clarity. We listen deeply for the true questions, trusting that the answer will unfold and reveal itself when the time is right. We become alert to the messages that come in subtle and surprising ways. We hold decisions lightly until the truth emerges. Discernment empowers us to be guided by Grace.

The Virtues Project

---

*Y*ou don't just wake up one day and say to yourself, "Today's the day I'm going to start speaking my truth." Well, that's not my experience of it, at least.

It's an ongoing journey of self-discovery that often starts with a nudge from intuition. In fact, I'd go so far as to say that intuition could just as easily be swapped for the word initiation, because more often than not it's intuition that starts the unravelling of the Gordian Knot that's holding you tight in your current way of being.

There are many parts to this unravelling that make it really tempting to not even go down this road. But, if you're like me, and I suspect because you're reading a book like this (that you are), then you don't really have a choice. There's a part of you buried so deep that is yearning for the light, that it fills you with a relentless drive to keep unravelling, to get to the truth and to live in that truth no matter how scary or hard it seems to be at times.

Even as a kid, I had this part of me that enabled me to see things from a different perspective to those around me. I could hear the parts of people's stories that were unspoken, read the room and know which groups of people it would be safe to be near, and which ones to avoid. I seemed to be able to access a deeper understanding of situations than what was apparent on the surface.

Back then my intuition was very finely tuned and worked well to help me navigate the ups and downs of a child who moved a lot and so was constantly thrown into the situation of creating new friends.

I can remember conversations with my parents when I came home despondent because "nobody likes me. They all hate me. They think I'm a weirdo."; to be told, "Don't be silly, how can you know what they're thinking?" True, I didn't know what was going on in their minds, but I could feel what was coming, or rather not coming, from their hearts. My intuition was flawless.

This brings me to the heart of the understanding needed to keep unpicking the weave of that knot in a way that brings you intact and at peace into the light.

IT'S NOT JUST YOUR IMAGINATION!

Intuition is an innate human ability. We are all born with it, just as we are born with our physical senses. Intuition provides another avenue for input into our intelligence centres to discern what is going on in our environment, so we can then determine the best way to respond. Once upon a time, in the days before language, intuition was part of our survival instincts. It was the faculty that enabled us to read the weather, pick up warning signs a life-saving split-second earlier, gauge the true intentions of strangers to the tribe, read the ebb and flow of life in the environment, find water hidden deep inside the Mother, and to grasp the vastness of the truth of our native interconnectedness.

How we do this is simple and yet very complex at the same time. Intuition is the bridge between our subtle body and our nervous system. Imagination is the lexicon our brain uses to interpret the information coming from the nervous system. Intuition and imagination working together bridge the gap between the ocean of rich language stored in our subconscious and our intellectual brain's ability to create meaning in every moment.

As I grew into adulthood, I clamped down on my intuition, burying it deep and chose to ignore it in favour of my analytical brain. I submitted to the societal programming acquired during school life and set out to get myself a good career, get married, have kids and live the Australian dream of success.

The skills I took for granted as a kid faded with lack of use, until only remnants remained.

GROOVE IS IN THE HEART

Journeying to the truth of who and what you are is like peeling an onion. You move through one layer, master the lessons contained there, only to discover yet another layer, shiny and new, waiting for you underneath; a whole new layer with all of its own unique lessons, and more often than not, a revision of some of the lessons learned before.

For me personally, reconnecting with intuition was part of a much bigger process; one that entailed acknowledging a powerful, secret part of myself that I'd been denying for many years; a part of myself that tolerated my intellectual choices for as long as it could before overwhelming soul-sickness drove me from the stifling, soul-destroying life I'd created for myself. It wasn't a fast transition and there were many moving parts including four young children, a husband, chronic illness, lots and lots of learning, and powerful self-realisations. It's a process that's still unfolding right now.

At the age of 42, I left a career in marketing with a secure income to immerse myself in the world of natural therapies and explored, with the open wonder of a child, the magic of the human body.

It was like letting a genie out of a bottle. That part of me that had been hidden for so long was finally free and there was no going back. The clues had been there all along. The way I operate, how I perceive the world, my decision-making process – I feel my way through life. I'd even had people tell me I wore my heart on my sleeve. But like any good quality ah-ha moment, it dawned on me only after I'd put enough space between myself and the high-pressure environment that was anathema to my soul.

Picking up a thread I thought I'd left behind forever in my twenties when I'd walked away from training in acupuncture, I returned to where I truly needed to be – in the realm of healing. At the same time, I worked hard to complete my qualifications in massage therapy, I was also introduced to Reiki.

What a gift this was – and still is!

Meeting Jan opened up a whole new world to me. One that invited a deep spirituality to blossom in my heart and mind. Being guided in the art of Reiki by this gifted teacher, helped me draw deeper connections between Reiki practice, the pathologies bodywork therapists encounter, and our role as a facilitator for healing to be experienced, rather than being an agent driving a particular healing outcome.

Becoming a part of Jan's teaching circle enabled me to connect with other Reiki practitioners whose main modalities were in alternative therapies such as Reflexology, Acupuncture, Naturopathy, Bowen Therapy, and Chiropractic. In this environment, my hunger for understanding was fed. It was a beautiful place to expand knowledge, exchange ideas, gain insight and receive advice when it was requested.

Rather than being an intangible, out-there, New Age kookiness, I found Reiki to be deeply grounded, anchored in the philosophy of Buddhism and Shintoism. It gave me a stable platform to continue my own personal and spiritual development. It also gave me a safe space with like-minded people as my intuitive ability continued to grow and I started tuning in and developing my higher senses.

I remember one afternoon at a gathering at Jan's place, noticing how relaxed and at home I felt. Even in the company of other practitioners who had many years of experience, I knew I belonged and that my input was respected. There was no sense of competition, no sense of having to defend or justify my contribution to the discussion. I suddenly found myself blurting out, "OMG, it is such a relief to be in a space where it's OK to start your sentence with 'I feel'!"

"Oh!" said Jan, giving a delighted laugh. "Tell us what you mean!"

"Well…" I started slowly, the revelation coming to me as I spoke. "I've just realised that for so long I've been working in an environment where everything is based on 'I think'. You had to be logical and justify your opinion or recommendation from an analytical space. It was all mind-based and ego driven. Whereas, in this space, I feel it's more about what comes from the heart, guided by intuition. Even just expressing your opinion or idea with the opening of 'I feel' and having that not only accepted, but the preferred frame of reference is a breakthrough for me."

I sat back letting the realisation wash through me, I had come home to a place of heart-based wisdom and understanding. All those times in staff meetings or presentations, when people had looked askance at me for expressing myself with 'I feel' rather than 'I think', I had been expressing my inner truth without realising it. I am a heart-based woman, I do feel things, I do make decisions based on feeling, AND, that is absolutely OK!

Owning this epiphany, letting this heart-based recognition settle deeply into my identity was a crucial moment in my spiritual development. It gave me license to embrace my mysterious nature and actively work with my intuitive capacity.

LOOKING FOR TRUTH IN ALL THE WRONG PLACES

As I journeyed deeper with Reiki, I also dived into exploring the realm of subtle energy. This led me into the quantum universe and an ongoing struggle to draw understanding from a field I just don't have any grounding in – quantum physics. For me at this point in my growth, it was important that I based my intuitive knowing and spiritual understanding on something that could be substantiated. I still felt the need to justify my understanding and the way I was working because it could be verified, or at the very least, be notionally supported, by frontier science.

All the while, though, my own inner wisdom was growing as my personal evidence bank of lived experience received constant, regular deposits.

My own body grew more and more sensitive to the flow of energy within. I was already well versed with the feeling of chi having had many years of regular acupuncture treatments. This body-knowing expanded to my yoga practice and mixed with my pranayama practice as my awareness continued building. I began to consciously take note of what I was experiencing in my body, how muscles responded and what certain sensations I started to recognise as shifting energy actually felt like. I could feel the energy in my body. Moreover, as I continued as a massage therapist I became acutely attuned to the movement of energy in my clients' bodies. Adding Reiki to the mix only heightened my acuity.

Using the rudimentary training in Traditional Chinese Medicine (TCM) I'd undertaken in my early 20's as a scaffold, I launched into learning as much as I could about the energy anatomy of the body. This tied in beautifully with my training in Reiki. Alongside what I was learning in Reiki, I explored a number of ancient Eastern philosophies bound in centuries of observation, recording, trial and error and profound Spiritual study. This led my understanding on a magical journey from the Web that has no Weaver through the concepts of Duality and Unity to an attempt to understand reality through the lens of quantum physics.

It was exciting, mind-boggling, re-affirming and deeply, deeply satisfying.

At the same time, I revisited my interest in Wicca and Paganism that I'd flirted with in my teens and early twenties, and surrendered to the call of myths and legends that had filled my childhood with such delight.

It all came together in a connection to my intuitive gift that I could comprehend, rationally debate and rest easily into. I relaxed into the connection with Spirit that I kept secret from the "real" world. I started sharing firstly with my mum, and then my husband that I connected with Spirit in the form of Archangel Michael, Ascended Master Kuan Yin, and the Goddess of Magik – Hecate. My rationale: understanding the Universe and everything in it, as energy. We are vibrational in nature, the 3D reality we live in on Earth is composed of energy vibrating at very low frequencies, and that these 'beings' are Archetypal energies vibrating at different frequencies that I was occasionally tuning into.

I loved exploring each of these areas, but there were two things wrong with my approach. One: I was still making decisions based on fear and not owning up to the truth of who and what I actually was. Two: I was looking "out there" for answers.

Even though things such as Angelic presence, power animals, symbols, and knowledge simply dropping in were once again an ordinary part of my day, my fear of being seen as a weirdo or tripped-out hippie kept me quiet and in a level of denial about a very important part of myself.

My fear of this external perception prompted me to stay hidden in the Spiritual Closet for a long time. After all, I'm an intelligent, articulate, university-educated woman and I come from a family of university-educated people. My father is a retired Civil Engineer in the Australian Army; my mother, a retired teacher of humanities – Senior English, History and Geography; and my younger brother is doing his damnedest to save the Great Barrier Reef with his PhD in Marine Biology. I couldn't possibly be cast as the Space Cadet of the family!

Acknowledging that fear and continuing on this pathway is one of the scariest, most painful things I think I've ever done. Scary because as well as the wealth of judgement that lives in our world at the moment, there's a shadowy overlay of memories of centuries of persecution echoing through the lineages of our ancestors, triggering a visceral fear of being seen. Facing that fear every day and choosing to continue isn't a picnic!

My journey has also been physically painful. That's mainly due to my stubbornness and lack of self-acceptance. Pain is a very good teacher!! If you're not listening, pain will get your attention. If you are subject to chronic pain, or episodes of pain, it's time to stop and tune in. Ask yourself, what is actually going on here? What am I missing?

THE TRUTH IS...

I am a Spiritual woman. I have a very clear perception of who and what I am and what that means for me and for the people around me. As such, it is incumbent on me to not only speak my truth, but to live it.

This means not only acknowledging but understanding and accepting my own divine light. It requires that I work with integrity, accessing the wisdom of my body and the centres of intelligence contained in mind, heart and gut in a fluid, balanced way that doesn't favour one over the other. It means being Awake in the present moment and fully integrated into body, mind, and spirit.

Harnessing your intuition to learn the Art of Discernment is the key to transcendence. One way or another, each of us reaches this point, where employing discernment brings us into Truth.

Truth isn't a fixed state that once reached no further work is required. Honouring Truth is a daily devotional practice of conscious Awakening. It requires constant application of the skills acquired through regular practices such as Yoga, Tai Chi, Transcendental Meditation and Mindfulness. Living your Truth then becomes a conscious choice enacted moment by moment.

We have the power of choice, always. We can open our eyes and learn to see through the illusion, including self-delusion, to know ourselves in Truth; or we can continue with our eyes closed oblivious to the Truth. It's as simple as moving from the head to the heart, or choosing love over fear. The truth is you can just as easily choose to Awaken into Heaven on Earth as you can choose to stay asleep in Hell.

LINDA EMSLIE

Like many other Lightworkers, Linda hid from her sacred contract for as long as she could. But no matter how many layers of denial and self-deception she hid under, the Light found her and ultimately called her forth!

Overcoming her fear of judgement, ridicule and not being valued Linda left the safety of her career in Marketing, transforming from Marketing Manager to Massage Therapist, to Reiki Master to Soul Connection Mentor.

An international best-selling author, and industry leader in doing business with the sacred feminine, Linda brings a unique blend of potent business skill with profound healing wisdom to empower other Spiritual business leaders with chronic illness to connect with their soul-aligned solutions for healing and business growth.

Linda lives in Darwin, Australia with her two youngest children, husband, border collie, cat and quirky chicken.

Connect with Linda online
Facebook:
www.facebook.com/transformwithlovlali
Website: www.lovlali.com

25

THE ART OF GRACE PUBLISHING HOUSE

*B*rigid Holder is a USA Today best-selling author, multiple times best-selling amazon author and publisher, professional businesswoman, and founder of The Art of Grace Publishing House. Before launching her publishing house, Brigid's many roles, both personal and professional, led her to pursue a path of personal development. A wife and mother to two teenage boys, she also helms the traditional family business as the Company Director.

Brigid started writing again in 2018 as a cathartic release. Delving deeper into her writing journey, she started to reap the benefits of publishing her own stories and became inspired to help other women do the same. The Art of Grace Publishing House, named after Brigid's beloved grandparents, now serves as a safe space for women to share their stories, express themselves and collaborate to magnify their voices. Publishing both solo and multi author books Brigid nourishes her clients with her mothering ways whilst mentoring them through practical steps to become more visible.

If you are ready to share your story, you can connect with Brigid here:

www.brigidholder.com/
Follow her on FB www.facebook.com/BrigidAuthorPublisher

GRATITUDE

Thank you for reading, we at The Art of Grace Publishing House love sharing womens stories. If you enjoyed this book, INTUITIVE – Speaking Her Truth please leave us a review on Amazon or send it to us at publishing@brigidholder.com

Other Multi Author Titles published by The Art Of Grace Publishing House:

INTUITIVE – Knowing Her Truth

F@#* Motherhood – Volume One

Made in United States
North Haven, CT
12 June 2022